THE INDIANS IN OKLAHOMA

Cheyenne Madonna. Courtesy of the Oklahoma Historical Society, Oklahoma City.

THE INDIANS IN OKLAHOMA

by Rennard Strickland

Oklahoma Image is a project sponsored by the Oklahoma Department of Libraries and the Oklahoma Library Association, and made possible by a grant from the National Endowment for the Humanities.

Library of Congress Cataloging in Publication Data

Strickland, Rennard.
  The Indians in Oklahoma.

  (Newcomers to a new land)
Bibliography: p.
  1. Indians of North America — Oklahoma — History.
I. Title.   II. Series.
E78.O45S84   976.6'00497   79-6717
ISBN 0-8061-1674-9
ISBN 0-8061-1675-7 pbk.

This Book is Written for
the Next Generation
of
Oklahoma Indians
Especially
James Bradley and Kathryn Gambill
and
Geoffrey and Jonathan Blackwell

Where the Indian passed in dignity,
disturbing nothing and leaving Nature as he
had found her; with nothing to record his
passage, except a footprint or a broken
twig, the white man plundered and wasted
and shouted; frightening the silences with
his great, braying laughter and his cursing.

—John Joseph Matthews,
Wah'Kon-Tah

CONTENTS

FOREWORD

This book is one of a series entitled "Newcomers to a New Land," which analyzes the role of the major ethnic groups that have contributed to the history of Oklahoma. Though not large in number as compared to some other states, immigrants from various European nations left a marked impact on Oklahoma's history. As in the larger United States, they worked in many economic and social roles that enriched the state's life. Indians have played a crucial part in Oklahoma's history, even to giving the state her name. Blacks and Mexicans have also fulfilled a special set of roles, and will continue to affect Oklahoma's future. The history of each of these groups is unique, well worth remembering to both their heirs and to other people in the state and nation. Their stories come from the past, but continue on to the future.

EDITORIAL COMMITTEE

H. Wayne Morgan, Chairman
University of Oklahoma

Douglas Hale
Oklahoma State University

Rennard Strickland
University of Tulsa

PREFACE

An Oklahoma Indian Calendar

This is a very personal book, a brief chronicle that attempts to capture the life and spirit of Oklahoma's Indian people. Because more than sixty-five Indian tribes, each with a distinctive history, have been located within the state's boundaries, this narrative can be only illustrative. Single occurrences must represent major events in the lives of dozens of tribes and thousands of individuals. The wealth of Oklahoma's Indian heritage is only suggested. Much of the depth and breadth of this truly remarkable story is left for the reader to explore in other, more detailed sources.

The principal task of any chronicler is to remember what is important in the life of a people. Oklahoma's Indian people have long recorded significant occurrences. On calendar sticks, in strands of wampum, on painted-hide calendars, the Indian tribal story has been told in such a way that important human events are not lost amid life's thousands of trivial details.[1]

History is more than dates and numbers. History is an act of remembrance. Each of us remembers our personal history in an episodic, pictorial calendar of the mind. We gauge time in terms of events—the year we moved across the country, the winter of the big freeze, the summer that the baby died, or the spring we won the high school championships. History is this kind of collective remembrance. Such Indian artifacts as the Kiowa calendar, a Comanche buffalo-hide robe, the Delaware Walum Olum sticks, the Kee-Too-Wah Cherokee wampum belts, or the Creek plates with their varied pictures, patterns, and symbols do for an Indian tribe what we do for ourselves when we measure and remember our lives.

This book is an attempt to remember Oklahoma Indian life in that pictorial, episodic way. Thousands of articles and books of formal history, anthropology, and ethnology have been written about Oklahoma Indian tribes. This narrative steps back and looks briefly and impressionistically at the people who are Oklahoma Indians.

In the process the reader is asked to think about the individual human beings whose lives are collectively the story of the Oklahoma Indian experience. The story of a nation is, after all, the story of a nation's people.

The Indian story is a poignant one. The Creek satirist Alexander Posey proclaimed "all my people are poets." The great Arapaho artist Carl Sweezy said, "Art is in the soul of the Indian." The prize-winning Kiowa novelist N. Scott Momaday called the Indian way of storytelling "an act of imagination" that is itself autobiographical. The Indian has recorded a way of life, a way of viewing, a way of knowing, a way of seeing, a way of living, and, most significantly, a way of surviving.[2]

In this book the story of Oklahoma's native peoples is cast as an Indian calendar. The narrative follows the seasons of a collective Indian experience. This calendar tells the Indian story in an Indian context: the story of the autumn of Indian nationhood; the long winter of white settlement and Oklahoma statehood, the spring of tribal renewal, and a modern Indian summer. Emmett Starr, the great Cherokee chronicler, complained to his friend and fellow historian Joseph Thoburn that "the two-gun historians" have distorted Oklahoma Indian history with "enough historical mistakes . . . to fill the maws of future two-gun historians for several decades."[3] In his letter to Thoburn, written fifty years ago, Starr reflected a traditional view of history that Oklahoma's Indian people continue to practice.

History is, in this Indian view, primarily the story of people recorded and remembered by people. Emotion and impression count in Indian remembrance in a way that dates and data never can. Indian history is thus the telling of the story of Indian people. The telling of that story involves more than recitation of the terms of the Atoka Agreement or the counting of the people massacred at the Washita. The Indians' stories, poems, pictures, and associated experiences speak volumes about life.

Among the ledger drawings—the sketches done by the Plains Indian prisoners at Fort Marion—is a picture executed by Wohow of a Kiowa warrior poised between a buffalo and a cow. "The Indian stands," Karen Peterson notes, "at the meeting of two cultures, the old on the left and the new on the right. Near one foot stand the myriad buffalo and tipi—the old food and lodging—while beneath the other foot lie the cultivated fields with a frame house adjoining, symbols of the new subsistence."[4] The Indian has turned his head away from the buffalo; he faces the cow, and his foot rests on the plowed earth.

One sees deeply into the inner world of the Indian in "The Gourd Dancer," N. Scott Momaday's poem to his grandfather Mammedaty (1880–1932):

> Mammedaty saw to the building of this house
> Just there, by the arbor, he made a camp in the old way.
> And in the evening when the hammers had fallen silent
> and there were frogs and orioleote in the black grass —
> and a low, hectic wind upon the pale, slanting plane
> of the moon's light — he settled deep down in his mind
> to dream. He dreamed of dreaming, and of the summer
> breaking upon his spirit, as drums break upon the
> intervals of the dance, and of the gleaming gourds.[5]

A stained-glass window adorns the altar of the chapel at Bacone Indian College, in Muskogee, Oklahoma. The work created by the distinguished Potawatomi artist Woody Crumbo has been seen by Baptist worshipers for almost four decades. What most of the Christians who sit in this Baptist church do not recognize is that Crumbo has executed a window in symbols and colors of the peyote movement, as if the chapel belonged to the Native American Church.

As one enters the Tulsa International Airport, there is a display from the Philbrook Art Center. In a case on the passenger's left hangs a painting by Creek-Cherokee artist Joan Hill completed during the days of the Vietnam War. *Wars and Rumors of Wars*, a meeting of the stoic Creeks gathered for council, conveys a sense of the contemporary relevance of the historic experiences of Oklahoma Indians.

Just before he died tragically in a truck accident, the Kiowa-Caddo artist T. C. Cannon finished a final lithograph. *Indian Princess Waiting for a Bus in Anadarko* portrays in a poignant and comic way the resilience and nobility of the Oklahoma Indian. Cannon's work speaks of survival in a way that a dozen sociological and economic surveys could never do.

A primary purpose of this book is to offset misconceptions about Indian people and Oklahoma's Indian heritage. Despite the Indians' compelling numbers and significant cultural influences, white Oklahomans know little about the history and the life of their state's Indian citizens. Stereotypes of Oklahoma Indians range from cardboard movie characters based upon the Sioux, Navajo, Blackfoot, and other non-Oklahoma Indians to recollections of oil-rich Creek-Seminoles and Osages of the 1920s abandoning a stalled Pierce Arrow. The prevailing image moves back and forth from the mixed-blood, "civilized" Indian society matron educated beyond her intellectual capacity to the lazy, shiftless public drunk. Such stereotypes of Oklahoma's contemporary Indian culture are more widespread than the ancient myths that the Indians themselves told. Somewhere between the popular cultural stereotypes and the massive volumes of scholarly Indian histories and anthropological studies, Oklahoma's flesh-and-blood Indian has been lost.

*   *   *

The writing of this book has been a challenge, a curse, and a rare opportunity. The effort forced me to think about something with which I had always lived. In short, I had to analyze, generalize, and summarize.

Fortunately, the University of Tulsa provides an ideal atmosphere for scholarly productivity. My duties as John W. Shleppey Research Professor of Law and History are designed to encourage work such as this book. Portions of the manuscript were written at President Twyman's country place deep in the heart of the old Cherokee Nation. I am grateful for the retreat as well as for his unwavering support of my work. Vice-Presidents John Dowgray and John Hayes of the University of Tulsa tolerate a good bit from me, and Al Soltow, Dean of the Graduate School, has listened to and provided funds for a number of my plans and theories. Tulsa Law School Deans Frank T. Read and Tommy L. Holland have understood and appreciated what I have tried to do. My friend and colleague Sue Titus Reid continues to share with me her enthusiastic commitment to scholarly productivity. Finally, I cannot imagine our university community or my own career without the warm encouragement, reasoned advice, and good friendship of Bill and Rita Bell.

An earlier version of this manuscript was read and suggestions for revisions were made by an informal Indian advisory board including Ruth Arrington, Ethel Krepps, Phil Lujan, Marvin Stepson, and Charles and Sharon Blackwell. Douglas Hale, of Oklahoma State University, reviewed the first draft of this effort. Others have shared with me their observations about Oklahoma Indians. They include Fred and LaDonna Harris, Betty Mealey, Charles Wilkinson, Reid Chambers, Jerry Muskrat, Scott Bradshaw, Kent Frizzell, P. Sam Deloria, Gene Crawford, Earl Boyd Pierce, W. W. Keeler, Dode

McIntosh, and John Vance. The work of *Tulsa Tribune* reporter Susan Witt on the contemporary Oklahoma Indian was a major resource. Arthur Silberman's fresh approach and continued scholarship have broadened my own understanding of the nature and importance of Oklahoma Native American painting. The Oklahoma Indian Affairs Commission also provided valuable material, as did the Bureau of Indian Affairs, particularly the Muskogee and Anadarko area offices.

For almost a decade my University of Tulsa colleague Garrick Bailey and I have carried on a dialogue about the Oklahoma Indian, and his ideas have reshaped many of my own. Much of the fieldwork reflected in this book was undertaken with my long-term collaborator and frequent co-author Jack Gregory. I have drawn heavily on our joint research and, as always, am much in his debt. This is the first book I have written since my father's death, and I am particularly sensitive to how much he and my mother have taught me about being an Oklahoma Indian.

It is to librarians that authors owe so much. McFarlin Library at the University of Tulsa is becoming a great research library where students of subjects as varied as Indian history and modern letters can find significant original materials. Guy Logsdon, Director of Libraries, and David Farmer, Director of Special Collections, have contributed to this work both as readers of the manuscript and as participants in the search for the data upon which the book is based. Finnegan Marsh, the first Curator of the Shleppey Collection, helped me find many of the nineteenth-century accounts that figure in this history. The late John W. Shleppey and his widow, Eunice Shleppey, have contributed greatly to this and future generations of students of the American Indian. The McFarlin library staff makes working here a pleasure.

Tulsa is a center for Indian research. The Thomas Gilcrease Institute of American History and Art is a premier musem and library whose staff now provides wonderful scholarly services. Both Fred Meyer, the Director of the Gilcrease, and Pat Edwards, the Curator of History, assisted in this book. The Philbrook Art Center's collection of Native American paintings is the finest in the world. Jay Wright and Chris Knop, of the Philbrook, helped me by providing access to the Indian collections there and also by supplying prints of many of the paintings.

Elsewhere in Oklahoma I have been assisted by Gilbert Fites, of Northeastern State University, the former Cherokee Seminary; Manon Adkins and Martha Blaine, of the Oklahoma Historical Society;

Peggy Denton, of the Five Civilized Tribes Museum; Marty Hager-strand, of the Cherokee Historical Society; and Jack Haley, Assistant Curator of the Western History Collections of the University of Oklahoma.

My greatest debt is to the Indian people of Oklahoma. The hospitality extended to me at powwows, church meetings, council sessions, and ball games speaks for the nature of Oklahoma Indianness. My questions have been not only tolerated but encouraged. I have also been well fed while I have been taught. Even among truly traditional peoples my work has been understood. Chief William Smith, Crosslin Smith, and the entire Kee-Too-Wah Council have shared with me much of their ancient and beautiful way. Many of the artists whose works are represented or discussed in this book have shared their thoughts and feelings with me. For several years Cecil Dick, the premier traditional Cherokee painter, attempted to teach me things that I am only now beginning to appreciate. Others, such as Joan Hill, Richard West, Virginia Stroud, Ben Harjo, Willard Stone, Fred Beaver, Terry Saul, David Williams, Woody Crumbo, Stephen Mopope, Robert Ansley, and Blackbear Bosin, have in our discussions inspired and informed my lust for their works.

Finally, I have reached the stage in my own work where I could not have undertaken a task such as this book without Rosemarie Spaulding. Her patience in retyping sections of my manuscripts would test even the most stoic of Oklahoma's Indians.

University of Tulsa   *Rennard Strickland*

Chapter 1

THE BRIGHT AUTUMN OF INDIAN NATIONHOOD

Blackbear Bosin's *Prairie Fire* captures the drama and spirit of early Indian life in Oklahoma. In this painting clouds of smoke and flames drive a herd of antelope, a pack of wolves, and two mounted Indian warriors across the broad and open plains. One senses in this flight that man, like beast, cannot escape the awesome power of nature. In yet another of Bosin's works, *Of the Owl's Own Telling,* a Plains warrior rests in the shadow of a great autumn moon and the stark bare branches of a tall tree. On his shoulder an owl sits, wings outspread and up against the moon. Perhaps the owl is sharing with the Indian some secret of their common struggle. The painting is testimony to the Indian's sense of awe and mystery, to a feeling of oneness with and respect for that earth which is now known as Oklahoma.[1]

In the days before the white settlement of Oklahoma this was a land whose vistas inspired in even the most urbane white visitor that same sense of awe. In 1832 the Prussian Count de Pourtalès recorded the exhilaration of an October morning in "the most beautiful stretches of forest that I have ever seen . . . magnificent, sparsely scattered trees . . . some bright green and others delicately shaped and turned red by the frost. The entire wood seemed to burst with many colors of autumn."[2] In the fall of 1832 the pristine majesty of early Oklahoma was observed by a "baroque caravan" of tourists made up of the American author Washington Irving; the British traveler, author, and biologist Charles Joseph Latrobe; the Prussian diplomat Count Albert-Alexandre de Pourtalès; and newly appointed United States Indian Commissioner Henry Ellsworth.[3] Much of what we know about Oklahoma in the early half of the nineteenth century comes from white travelers, soldiers, hunters, and artists who came

1

west to observe what was known as the great Indian wilderness. They portrayed the autumns of Oklahoma native life on this "rocky, rolling prairie watered by numerous streams and colored blood red by sumacs."[4]

To the white as well as the Indian this land was a paradise, a wild and beautiful place "as if set off by the hand of art."[5] Oklahoma's prairie interior was "the debatable grounds of warring and vindictive tribes," a land described by Irving as "a vast tract of uninhabited country . . . of great grassy plains, interspersed with forests and groves, and clumps of trees, and watered by the Arkansas, the grand Canadian, the Red River, and their tributary streams."[6] These were the lands of "savage conflicts," where "still roamed the elk, the buffalo, and the wild horses in all their native freedom" and no Indians "presume to erect a permanent habitation within its borders." A horseman could ride for days "where there is neither to be seen the log house of the white man, nor the wigwam of the Indian."[7] The fields "teemed with quail, polecats, and turkeys," and "deers, bucks and fawns bounded livelier through the grass, underbrush, and woods until their white hindquarters disappeared into the mysterious forests and valleys beyond the hills."[8]

The free spirit of the place inspired Count Pourtalès to write in his personal diary that "if ever I settle in America, it will be in this area, the only place in the United States which offers a romantic way of life as well as absolute independence. I would surround myself with a double rampart of Osages to protect me against the Americans, these commercial Thebans of the New World. . . . It would be a beautiful life."[9] For the Indian too it was a beautiful life. For a brief moment in time Indian life in Oklahoma seemed free and independent. The white had brought horse and gun to the Indian but had only begun to use them to bind him to a fixed abode and to the farmer's fields.

This time before the American Civil War and the 1867 Treaty of Medicine Lodge is remembered as the Golden Age of the Oklahoma Indian. For many Indians this age followed the brutal, nearly genocidal expulsion from their original homelands. Such irony pervades much of Oklahoma's Indian life. The present Indian nature of the state is the result not of aboriginal Indian choice but of white policy. Most Oklahoma Indians opposed coming to the state. Oklahoma's Indian people are largely descendants of nineteenth-century emigrants who had been driven by whites from almost every other section of the country. More bitterly ironic, Indians found in Oklahoma a quiet haven. Eventually they came to love this land, and in the end it too was taken from them.

Generalizing about the coming of the Indian to Oklahoma is not easy. Tribes came at different times and for different purposes (see map 1). Divisions of the same tribe were often split by migration. Oklahoma was historically a great and open hunting ground through which passed many native peoples. State boundaries and formal tribal borders were unknown before white occupation. Even the rigid recognition of formal tribal units was a political concept borrowed from the whites. Certainly the fee-simple ownership of land with its feudal property implications was foreign to the mind of the aboriginal American. Furthermore, in a society where splinter factions were free to move away from the main body of a tribe, portions of groups as large as the Seneca or the Osage or the Cherokee might be settled in several states as well as in Indian Territory. Other tribes might never be settled anywhere, in the traditional European sense, but rather ranged from the plains of Texas into the Rocky Mountains and beyond.

Only a few of the presently identifiable Oklahoma tribes were within the state when the Europeans arrived.[10] Fewer than half a dozen of Oklahoma's tribes are indigenous.[11] Very early ancestors of the Oklahoma Indians, such as Plainview, Clovis, and Folsom man, as well as more immediate paleolithic ancestors, had disappeared.[12] The great prehistoric Indian civilizations with their mounds and their monumental art, such as those unearthed at Spiro in the 1930s, were gone when the first white explorers came to Oklahoma.[13] Quapaw and Caddoan ancestors of the Wichitas and Caddoes by that time had settled on this land with their village farming culture. Tribes like the Osage hunted in these domains, and nomadic bands such as the Plains Apaches and the Comanches followed the migratory herds across the state. To appreciate the nature of Indian settlement within the state, distinctions among hunting, migration, and permanent residence must be made. Further, one must appreciate the concept of a home base to which roving tribes might return with some regularity.

The major thrust of Indian settlement in Oklahoma was the result of white policy: formal negotiations; informal counsel, bribery, and threats; and military force. As early as 1803, Thomas Jefferson had spoken of a permanent Indian area or territory beyond the boundaries of white settlement.[14] Since before the founding of the nation, Indian tribes had been driven from white areas by both war-

3

fare and treaty negotiations. By various inducements and by the application of brute force more than sixty Indian tribes originally from other states were ultimately removed to and resettled in Oklahoma. This process "conformed in no phase or degree to any pattern," for "there was an infinite variety of methods, experiences, and details."[15] Removal was undertaken, particularly at the turn of the century for the northern Indians of Ohio, Indiana, Illinois, and New York, without plan or experience. Thus many once-powerful tribes — Shawnee, Sac and Fox, and Potawatomi — were fragmented, lost, or reduced in station before their arrival in the Indian Territory.

Voluntary migrations and inducements by treaty settled portions of such tribes as the Senecas, Quapaws, Osages, Shawnees, Choctaws, Creeks, and Cherokees in Oklahoma before full implementation of Andrew Jackson's Indian Removal Act in the 1830s. In these earlier removals there seemed to be no system or order, but the government progressed "with candor or guile, by arguments, threats, or cajolery, by appealing to corruptible chiefs, by gorging the Indians at councils with food and drink — whatever the exigencies suggested."[16] Some tribes were moved several times before they reached Oklahoma. Many tribal groups, sensing the futility of resistance to removal, sought a negotiated compromise that avoided the brutality of a forced military march to their new country. Thus by the early 1830s there were established tribal governments in Oklahoma of "old settler" or "western" factions of the Choctaws, Creeks, and Cherokees, as well as separate political subdivisions of groups like the Osages, whose greatest numbers would not come to Oklahoma until much later. For example, the Senecas in 1831 exchanged land in Ohio's Sandusky Valley for 67,000 acres north of the western Cherokees, while a short time later another group of Senecas and Shawnees received a similar Indian Territory tract. In 1833 a band of Quapaws moved from the Red River to lands north and east of the Cherokees.

The tragedy of the removal of almost sixty thousand members of the great southern nations — the Creeks, Cherokees, Choctaws, Chickasaws, and Seminoles — is known as the "Trail of Tears" because in the brutal forced migration as many as one-fourth of the Indians died from exposure and exhaustion.[17] The agony of this experience is etched in the consciousness of not only the Five Civilized Tribes but non-Indian Oklahomans as well. These southern tribes in turn had been joined in Oklahoma by other tribes, particularly northern woodland peoples, whose experiences were often as disastrous (see map 2).

4

Between the end of the Civil War and the opening of Oklahoma's Unassigned Lands in 1889 the number and nature of Indian tribes permanently living in Oklahoma changed (see map 3). The many plains and woodland tribes who joined the earlier inhabitants brought a diversity of Indian culture not present in any other state. In the northeast corner of the state the Peorias, Modocs, Ottawas, Shawnees, and Wyandots joined the Senecas and the Quapaws. In the northeastern and central portions of the state were the Osages, the Kaws, the Pawnees, the Tonkawas, the Poncas, the Otos and Missouris, the Sac and Foxes, the Iowas, the Kickapoos, the Potawatomis, and the Shawnees. Dominating the eastern half of the state and spilling into the west were Cherokees, Creeks, Choctaws, Chickasaws, and Seminoles. In the western part of the state, around the military outposts of Fort Reno and Fort Sill, the great tribes of the plains were ultimately located. The Comanche, Kiowa, and Apache lands bordered on Texas. The Wichita and Caddo tribes nestled between this reservation and the reservation lands of the Cheyennes and Arapahos.

Ironically, more has been written and less is known about the history and culture of these Oklahoma tribes than about any other group of Native Americans. As many as 600,000 present-day Oklahoma citizens are of Indian descent, and the percentage of Oklahomans identifying themselves as Indians went up by more than a third between the 1960 and the 1970 United States censuses.[18] Yet within the state of Oklahoma there remains a widespread perception that the Indian and the Indian's culture is vanishing. "Non-Indians . . . are more ignorant of the Indian than the Indian is of them," according to a recent study of the population of Oklahoma City. "This is so because the majority of whites and blacks have had little personal contact with individual Indians and [even] that has been extremely superficial."[19]

The contemporary facts are unmistakably clear.[20] Oklahoma has more Indians than any other state in the Union. It has more separate tribal groups historically associated with the state and more currently recognized tribes than any other state. A higher percentage of its population is Indian, and that population is more widely distributed among the state's counties than in Arizona, New Mexico, or the Dakotas. Indians who once owned all the land in the state now have a greatly reduced land base, the lowest income level, and the highest unemployment rate of any group in the state. Today more Oklahoma Indians are participating in more Indian-sponsored activities than in

5

any period since statehood. The number of Oklahoma Indians is increasing. Indian tribes are again functioning as political and economic units, electing officials, administering programs, and dispensing justice.

The state is truly what Chief Allen Wright's name for it, Okla Homma, conveys in a free translation from the Choctaw—"Home of the Red People." More than sixty-seven tribes and bands have been located within the state and twenty-nine of them continue to be recognized.[21] In 1970 more than 96,000 Indians identified themselves to the United States census.[22] There are 100,000 sociocultural Indians, 220,000 persons recognized by the Bureau of Indian Affairs as legal Indians, and 600,000 Oklahomans of Indian descent.[23] Tulsa and Oklahoma City rank second and third behind Los Angeles in Indian population within city boundaries.[24] The sixty-five-mile trade radius of Tulsa constitutes the highest nonreservation concentration of Indians anywhere in the world.[25]

The great diversity of Oklahoma's Indian population is lost in these statistics. More than the plains tribes or the Five Civilized Tribes reside in Oklahoma. Among the state's larger tribal groups are peoples as varied as the Poncas and the Apaches, the Comanches and the Choctaws. With urban migration Indians from at least forty other non-Oklahoma tribes have recently moved to the state. More and more of Oklahoma's Indians have ancestors from two to four or more tribes. An Osage-Cherokee, a Kiowa-Miami, a Creek-Omaha is not unusual. The current generation is producing children who are such combinations as Choctaw-Ponca-Cheyenne-Delaware or Cherokee-Osage-Omaha-Creek-Apache.

Even among members of the same tribe there are great cultural and personal differences. Today as many as 10,000 Cherokees speak their native tongue in a tribe that began adopting white cultural variants in the eighteenth century.[26] While Oklahoma United States Senator Robert L. Owen (1907–25), an enrolled Cherokee, was engaged in the co-authorship of the Federal Reserve Act of 1913, the Cherokee Kee-Too-Wahs were reading the ancient wampum belts and feeding the sacred fire with the blood of a white rooster.[27]

Oklahoma has historically been a land of great contrasts between and among Indian people. Contemporary distinctions within the same or among different tribal groups are reflective of similar differences among Indians even in the age before widespread settlement of whites within the state. Nineteenth-century accounts of travelers, Indian tribal documents, missionary diaries, government negotiations, military reports, and trader journals clearly establish that there has never been a single, unified Oklahoma Indian culture.

For convenience Oklahoma's Indian tribes are often grouped into broad categories, such as the Five Civilized Tribes and the Plains Indians, or into semigeographic, quasi-cultural divisions, such as Hunters of the Plains, Plains Farmers, Woodland Peoples, or Northern and Southern Woodland, Prairie, Plains, and High Plains Indians. Such artificial subdivisions are meaningful only when the broad cross-cultural similarities and the genuinely unique aspects of each tribe are remembered. Choctaws and Seminoles, two "civilized" tribes, are in major respects culturally distinct, just as are the plains groups, such as the Kiowas and the Arapahos. To appreciate these varied cultures and what the Oklahoma Indian lost after the coming of white immigrants, one must understand the nature of Indian life on the prairie and in the woodland before the Civil War and the Treaty of Medicine Lodge. It is the culture of this golden age to which Oklahoma's modern Indians look with nostalgia.

The traditional Indian culture of Plains tribes such as the Cheyennes, Arapahos, Kiowas, and Comanches is familiar to most Americans. Their seemingly free and independent life has come to symbolize Oklahoma's Native peoples. These were hunter cultures, uniquely varied in many respects. But each depended on the existence of both open lands that could be freely roamed and an abundant supply of wild game. Plains Indian thought, culture, and organization were complex. At the heart of it was a civil, military, and religious structure that preserved law and order, provided security, and assured economic and social well-being. It was a life intimately tied to the earth and the natural cycles of life.

One gets a sense of the dominance of the seasons and an understanding of the oneness with natural elements from the naming of the months of the Cheyenne year.[28] The importance of the buffalo is also obvious from the calendar. The year begins with the moons just before winter, and typical months are "The moon the leaves fall off," "the moon the buffalo cow's fetus is getting larger," "the moon the wolves run together," "the moon the ducks come," "the moon the grass commences to get green," "the moon the corn is planted," "the moon the buffalo bulls are fat," and "the moon that plums get red."

The substance and rhythm of Kiowa life suggests what much of Prairie and Plains Indian life was like in the days before the reservation. Early pictures on the Kiowa calendar convey a precise and

7

vivid history of an Indian way at once free and ranging in scope but precisely and intently directed. Events are represented on this painted hide by pictographic symbols that recount major occurrences in a civilization nomadic in nature but stable in ritual. In examining the Kiowa calendar migration suggested by the Sun Dance location pictures, James Mooney concluded that by 1832 present-day Oklahoma had become a home base for the Kiowas.[29]

The pictographs on the Kiowa calendar show both winter and summer encampments with particularly strong descriptions of the central role of the Sun Dance, showing the location or unusual events that distinguished this summer religious celebration. For example, the summer of 1850 was Chinaberry Sun Dance because it was held near a thicket of these trees a short distance from Fort Supply; 1851 was Dusty Sun Dance because a strong wind on the north bank of the Canadian kept the air filled with dust. We also see from the 1851 drawing that at the Dusty Sun Dance a group of Pawnees stole from the center pole of the medicine lodge the offerings that had been hung as a sacrifice. The Kiowas proudly record the revenge of the affront with an attack on the Pawnees.

Not only the ceremonial but also the daily life of this Plains tribe is vividly recorded on the Kiowa calendar. A man covered with red spots symbolized the winter of 1839–40, called "smallpox winter" when the Osages introduced the disease that spread to the Kiowas, Apaches, and Comanches, killing large numbers. The symbol for the disease was repeated in the winter of 1861–62. The winter of 1833–34 was distinguished as "the winter the stars fell" because of a memorable meteoric display that came while the tribe was camped on the Elm Fork of the Red River in present Greer County, Oklahoma. One sees the less dramatic nature of this life from "muddy traveling winter," "winter that they dragged the head," and "winter that they left their tipis behind." Poignant suggestions of what was yet to come are the pictures of "summer of sitting with legs crossed and extended," "winter that Wrinkled-Neck built a trading post," and "sitting summer of worn-out horses." By 1882 the calendar showed "no Sun Dance because no buffalo," and 1887 ironically pictures "buffalo bought for Sun Dance."

George Catlin, the frontier artist, traveling on the western prairie in 1834, came upon what appeared to be a typical plains encampment. He described "a great Camanchee village" of "six or eight hundred skin-covered lodges, made of poles and buffalo skins" with a population of "thousands of wild inmates, with horses and dogs, and wild sports and domestic occupations." Catlin's paintings said much about nomadic Indian life on Oklahoma's western plains and prairies. "These people," Catlin noted, "living in a country where buffaloes are abundant, make their wigwams more easily of their skins, than of anything else; and with them find greater facilities of moving about . . . when they drag them upon poles attached to their horses, and erect them again with little trouble in their new residence."[30]

Catlin captured much of the human dimension of Plains Indian life, particularly the hunting and the games and the racing. Horse racing was "a constant and almost incessant exercise and their principal mode of gambling." To Catlin the Plains warriors were "the most extraordinary horsemen that I have seen yet in all my travels," who "the moment they mount their horses . . . seem at once metamorphosed, and surprise the spectator with the ease and elegance of their movements."[31] In a sense this free and roaming Indian hunter life rested on native adaptation to the introduction by whites of the modern horse. To Washington Irving a mounted Indian hunter on a prairie was like a cruiser on the oceans, "perfectly independent of the world."[32] The French traveler Victor Tixier found that "large herds of horses are the real riches of the prairie savages" and concluded that "the horse saves the savage."[33]

The migration of a full Indian village provided a great contrast to the "wonderful art . . . and feats of horsemanship." Catlin recorded that in the process of moving

several thousands were on the march, and furnished one of those laughable scenes which daily happens, where so many dogs, and so many squaws, are travelling in such confused mass: with so many conflicting interests, and so many local and individual rights to be pertinaciously claimed and protected. Each horse drags his load, and each dog . . . also dragging his wallet on a couple of poles; and each squaw with her load, and all together (not withstanding their burdens) cherishing their pugnacious feelings, which often bring them into general conflict, commencing usually amongst the dogs, and sure to result in fisticuffs of the women; whilst the men, riding leisurely on the right or the left, take infinite pleasure in overlooking these desperate conflicts, at which they are sure to have a laugh, and in which, as sure never to lend a hand.[34]

The movable house, the tipi, symbolized nomadic Plains Indian life, and at the same time provided family stability, continuity, and tribal pride. Long after Catlin's visit among the "skin covered lodges" Carl Sweezy, the Cheyenne-Arapaho artist, recalled living in a tipi village:

9

Winter or summer our village made a beautiful sight when the sun went down, with the crossed poles pointing up into the dark sky and the fire in the center of each lodge turning it into a cave of light. . . . Sometimes a bell twinkled, where a herd of ponies grazed; sometimes dogs barked, before they settled down for the night; often there was a drum beating, deep and slow or fast and sharp. Sometimes there was the sound of a flute playing two or three notes over and over, or of men and women singing around a campfire. In the distance . . . the prairie stretched away in the darkness, mile after mile.[35]

Traveling on past the Comanches, Catlin came to the banks of the Red River, where a band of Pawnees was encamped. Their town illustrated the subtle diversity among the Indians who ultimately settled in Oklahoma. "We found," Catlin recorded, "a very numerous village, containing some five or six hundred wigwams, all made of long prairie grass, thatched over poles which are fastened in the ground and bent in at the top; giving to them, in distance, the appearance of straw beehives." Colonel Dodge and the dragoons who accompanied the expedition were surprised to find "these people cultivating extensive fields of corn (maize), pumpkins, melons, beans, and squashes; so, with these aids, and an abundant supply of buffalo meat, they may be said to be living very well."[36]

In addition to planting corn and squash, the Pawnees, like other tribes as diverse as the Osages and the Cheyennes, hunted the buffalo. In early Oklahoma the herds were often so thick that the hills were black with oceans of the bison, truly a sea of buffalo.[37] About the buffalo there was something "diabolical" and "whimsical," "a mixture of the awful and the comical."[38] Writers and painters were struck by the hypnotic, mesmerizing quality of the eyes of the great beast. There is little wonder that this animal who could supply almost all the tribes' needs seized the legends and life of so many Indian people.

The life of the hunter Indian was, as Count Pourtalès observed, "made up of contrasts." Depending on the outcome of the chase, "one day there is the abundance of Canaan, the next day there is famine." The life thus "mixes the extremes of joyful possession and deprivation, voluptuousness and austerity." It was a life that Europeans could easily romanticize, as the count did in comparing the Osage's existence "to the paintings of a great master, a mixture of deep shadows and points of light."[39]

Indian life on the western buffalo prairies and the open plains contrasted sharply with the settled, rural life of the Five Civilized Tribes who were transplanted in the early nineteenth century from the South to Oklahoma's eastern streams, forested hill, and scrub-oak country.[40] Even today there is a difference in look and feel as one passes from east to west. Washington Irving, in the openness of the western prairie, gazing at the stars at night, felt as though he were "watching . . . from the deck of a ship at sea, when at one view we have the whole cape of heaven."[41] By contrast, in the forest Irving felt "overshadowed by lofty trees, with straight, smooth trunks, like stately columns; and as the glancing ray of the sun shown through the transparent leaves, tinted with many-colored hues of autumn . . . was reminded of the effect of sunshine among the stained glass windows and clustering columns of a Gothic cathedral."[42]

The ways in which these southeastern Indians—Cherokees, Choctaws, Chickasaws, Creeks, and Seminoles—adapted, in varying degrees, a portion of white civilization to their own needs was fascinating. Known officially as "civilized," this group of Indians early determined that survival required adaptation. They believed that Indian tribes could prevail only by outsmarting the whites, and that required the use of white institutions. Their attitude was summarized in a letter to the missionary Daniel Sabin Buttrick in which Cherokee Chief Charles Hicks argued that the abandonment of many old tribal ways represented the "conviction that their very existence as a people depends upon it."[43]

Life among the woodland Indians, particularly the Five Civilized Tribes, focused not on the open hunt but on the closed field. Indian acculturation—what the white man called civilization—was reflected in the nature of their settlements and agricultural economy. The Choctaws, Cherokees, Creeks, Chickasaws, and Seminoles, as southern woodland peoples, had been settled village dwellers, farmers as well as hunters, for longer than white men had been in the New World. When they were driven to Oklahoma, they naturally sought fertile, well-watered lands on which to rebuild and reshape their traditional civilization. Although their fee-simple, patent tribal domains extended across the entire state, these tribesmen clustered most tightly near their eastern borders.

Captain John Stuart, the military engineer who spent most of his career building Indian Territory forts and roads, described the early Oklahoma Cherokees as settled on individual farms along rivers such as the Arkansas, Neosho, and Illinois and their tributaries and along the small streams running through the country.[44] A similar pattern of clustered river-and-stream settlement was followed by the Choctaws, Chickasaws, Creeks, and Seminoles. Stuart noted that once in Oklahoma the Choctaws "ceased to rove, or to live in villages, as was their ancient custom" but "settled on farms dispersed over the country."[45] In addition to these Indian farmers, who settled on relatively small plots, an Indian plantation class owned black slaves and followed the pattern of large-scale southern agriculture, planting vast acreage to produce crops for sale to the non-Indian market.[46] Land was abundant and free for all to use in whatever amounts they could cultivate.

Each of the Five Civilized Tribes tried to adapt its traditional ways and to preserve its Indian nationhood. With his invention of the Cherokee syllabary Sequoyah provided his tribe with almost universal literacy in its tribal language.[47] Four of the five tribes adopted and published written constitutions based on many of the principles of Anglo-American law.[48] What emerged from these unique experiments were independent Indian republics that supported not only a native farmer class but also an educated merchant and professional class. The tribes established public schools conducted in both English and the Indian languages and published millions of pages of tribal newspapers, religious tracts, schoolbooks, laws, pamphlets, and political broadsides.[49] At the same time numbers of young men and some women were attending eastern schools, and great numbers of young women and men were being educated at tribal and missionary schools.

In short, the Five Civilized Tribes borrowed what suited them from white society while retaining much of their distinctively Indian culture. The ownership of land in common and the shared use of tribal resources were continued. Many of the most important elements of tribal culture, such as respect for the land, shared obligation for the welfare of fellow tribesmen, and regard for the rights of women, were preserved. Other traditions merged in a society that provided a maximum of freedom to pursue either traditional Indian or white cultural variations. The results, at least in the so-called Golden Age before the Civil War, was a unique adaptation, a cultural merger that existed nowhere else in the Indian country.[50]

General Ethan Allen Hitchcock's detailed record of his 1841–42 visit to the Five Civilized Tribes provides a vivid picture of daily life in every class of each of the tribes.[51] Hitchcock portrayed Indians interacting with traders, missionaries, federal agents, and cavalry officers. Commerce, primarily in the hands of mixed-blood native merchants, ranged from the management of salt works to running boardinghouses and operating trading posts and gristmills. Some Cherokees, Creeks, and Seminoles shipped merchandise on steamboats up the Arkansas River and then loaded it on horses and headed out on the prairies to trade with the hunter Indians. Others, particularly the Choctaws and the Chickasaws, operated sophisticated trading houses for members of their own tribes, the military, nomadic Indians, and even whites from beyond their borders. Village dwellers in small communities like Choteau, Doaksville, and Tahlequah employed blacksmiths and distributed goods, including salt from the local salines. These Indian towns would swell in population and activities like a farm town after harvest or a county seat when the council met or an agent visited.

At almost all times in all the nations there were Indian celebrations, dances, and games. There were old-fashioned southern balls where "they danced a certain reel, incessantly, more complicated than the old Virginia Reel" and "broke down two fiddlers and ended with a third."[52] There was also the traditional Creek busk where "the fire is kept alive . . . and at the green corn dance it is renewed" and "the women have terrapin shells tied below their knees, loaded with peas," and "the men and women dance together" what was called by the Creeks their "buffalo dance."[53] Many white missionaries competed by holding Sunday preaching and public worship for the converted and the hangers-on. Horse racing, and its associated gambling was without question the most popular sport in all the Five Civilized Tribes.

The most dramatic sporting activity, however, was the Choctaw ball play. The competition, played either barehanded or with curved stickball racquets, was recalled by almost every visitor to the nation and painted by most frontier artists. George Catlin happened upon the Choctaws when they had gathered at "a sort of season of amusement . . . with horse racing, dancing, wrestling, foot racing, and ball playing."[54] At a Choctaw ball game "six or eight hundred or a thousand young men . . . engage in a game of ball, with five or six times that number of spectators, surrounding the ground, and looking on." Catlin eulogized the scene with its "hundreds of Nature's most beautiful models, denuded, and painted various colors, running and leaping into the air, in all the most extravagant and varied forms, in the desperate struggle for the ball." To the artist, he explained, it seemed the American aboriginal equivalent of the Olympian games or the Roman Forum.

There were major distinctions not only among tribes but also among full-bloods and mixed-blood members within each tribe. Rose Cottage, the elegant columned antebellum mansion of Chief John

Ross contrasted sharply with the more common hewed-log cabins, each with its dog-trot porch, exemplified by the one-room cabin Sequoyah built.[55] Both Hunter House near Park Hill and Sequoyah's cabin outside Sallisaw still stand. Other surviving examples of the pre-statehood architecture from the Five Civilized Tribes illustrate similar substantial though less extravagant homes.[56] But few of the small huts where the poorest Indians "lived miserably" survive.

The contrasts among the Five Tribes were also great. Although sometimes treated as a single administrative unit, the Cherokees, Creeks, Choctaws, Chickasaws, and Seminoles differed in many respects.[57] Creek government was a confederation composed of varied tribes and bands of primarily Muskogean-language peoples with the tribal town as the basic political unit. Representatives in the Creek House of Warriors and the House of Kings were chosen by towns that might retain their Yuchi or Natchez traditions. The Cherokees divided their nation into seven geographic districts with no national representation by units such as towns. Within the Creek tribe each of the towns retained considerable autonomy in social attitudes and even in law enforcement, while a greater national uniformity was demanded by the Cherokees.

In 1836, Captain John Stuart observed these differing tribal outlooks, such as the Cherokee and Choctaw attitudes toward speaking the English language. "More than one-half of the Cherokees understand something of the English language," he noted, "but none will use it in the presence of strangers, unless they can speak it free of their native dialect." In the Choctaw Nation "they will speak every word that they know whenever it is necessary."[58] Again, in contrast, the Choctaws had "more than double as many schools as there were in any other nation of Indians within the United States."[59] Paradoxically, while "fewer of the Choctaws crossed with white blood," the ancient Choctaw clan divisions had "long been neglected," while among the intermarried Cherokees traditional clan structure flourished.[60] Contrasting the number of mixed bloods among the Cherokees, Chickasaws, and Choctaws with those among the Creeks, another military figure concluded, "There are not many among the Creeks and the relative condition of the tribe is distinctly marked by that fact."[61]

Although the degree of acculturation varied, in their cultural adaptation the Five Civilized Tribes preserved a particularly strong sense of mutual respect between traditionalists, who maintained much of the old religion intact, and acculturationists, many of whom became Christians. The tribal identification was so strong that an eighth-blood Cherokee, John Ross, led the full-blood faction while a full blood, Major Ridge, led the mixed bloods. Among the Five Civilized Tribes, full blood and mixed blood, traditionalists and acculturationists united in opposition to pressures to weaken tribal government and surrender Indian lands. One observer noted in 1841 that

the whites' sons and their sons' sons born among the Cherokees of Cherokee blood have no sympathy with the whites but are devoted in their attachment to the country of their birth. Their number has become so great and they are so completely identified with the natives that if any man could conceive the desire to separate them from those of full blood, it would be impossible to succeed.[62]

The history of the Five Tribes might be written as a united but futile effort to block the series of treaties and acts that surrendered more and more of the tribal domain and led to removal and ultimately to the abolition of the independent Indian nations by merger into the state of Oklahoma.

In absolute numbers the Five Civilized Tribes and the Plains Indians historically constituted the largest blocs of Oklahoma Indians, but there were and still are other important, interesting, and colorful Oklahoma tribes, such as the Sac and Foxes, the Osages, the Potawatomis, the Quapaws, the Delawares, the Kickapoos, the Senecas, and the Shawnees. In addition, remnants of such tribes as the Catawbas, the Natchez, and the Biloxis and such tribes as the Yuchis and the Hitchitis were integrated into Oklahoma Indian governments, particularly those of the Choctaws, the Creeks, and the Cherokees. During his tour of Indian Territory in the 1840s, Major Ethan Allen Hitchcock concluded that "fragments of Indian tribes are scattered in every direction"[63]

The Osages attracted particular attention. Irving called them "the finest looking Indians I have ever seen in the West."[64] Catlin thought the Osages were "the tallest race of men in North America and "at the same time well-proportioned" and "good looking."[65] They were often praised for their steadfast resistance to white influence. Osages lived "near the borders of civilization" but "rejected everything of civilized customs."[66] In the nineteenth century they refused to "lay by their simple Indian garb, or to lose the habits of the hunter and the warrior."[67]

The circle of Indian life was represented by the Osage year.

During the fall the Osage family feasted on corn and beans, dried pumpkins, and dried meats. The autumn hunt extended from September to about Christmas. From January through March the hunters remained in the villages with occasional short hunting excursions. Spring hunting began in late February or, more generally, March, with bear and beaver hunts that continued until the spring planting. In May the men set forth on the summer hunt.[68] Like the Cheyennes, the Osages conveyed a sense of the natural events in their world by their seasonal reckoning. The months of autumn are "deer-hiding moon," "deer-breeding moon," and "coon-breeding moon." Winter contains "baby-bear moon," "single moon by himself," and the last month of the cold season, "light-of-day returns moon." The months of spring are "just doing moon," "planting moon," and "little-flower-killer moon." The summer months are "buffalo-pawing-earth moon," "buffalo-breeding moon," and "yellow flower moon."[69]

The journal of the Union Mission in 1821–22 described the nature of the work cycle in traditional Osage life. "Their females," the missionaries noted, "perform the labor" while the "men do the hunting, go to war, and much of the time having nothing to do, while the laborious wife or daughter is packing wood across the plain or bringing water or planting corn and the like." When accompanying hunting parties, "the women take care of [the men's] horses, prepare their encampments, in short do all the drudgery, while the men spend their leisure time in smoking and diversion."[70] The missionaries as outside observers of the culture did not understand the power and influence the Osage women seemed to have. For all of Osage society, including the relations between the sexes, functioned in the shadow of a religious system that colored every aspect of hunting, planting—indeed, of life and its living.

Faced with a changing world, even the nineteenth-century Osages were forced to change. Through it all they retained what one of their number, John Joseph Mathews, called "a beauty, an order, a perfection, a mystery far above my comprehension."[71] The "Song of the Maize" suggested the Osage sense of mystery and awe as spring is awakening the earth following the earth's winter death. The song seeks help from the mysterious one crossing the fields. Spirits of the Osage dead speak in this song as the smoke or early morning mist rises from the fields where Osage women are planting corn:

Amid the earth, renewed in verdure,
Amid rising smoke, my grandfather's footprints
I see, as from place to place I wander,
The rising smoke I see as I wander.
Amid all forms visible, the rising smoke
I see, as I move from place to place.

Amid all forms visible, the little hills in rows
I see, as I move from place to place.

Amid all forms visible, the spreading blades
I see as I move from place to place.

Amid all forms visible, the light day
I see as I move from place to place.[72]

Viewpoints and problems shared by Oklahoma Indian tribes are often lost in their cultural diversity and in their own internal dissension. And yet even before the opening of Indian lands to white settlement, these tribes reacted to similar challenges and faced many of the same dangers from their common white and Indian enemies. As early as 1824 the tribes faced an invasion of commercial hunters and an assault on native game. General Matthew Arbuckle reported two thousand hunters systematically killing fur-bearing animals in order to sell their peltries.[73]

The white challenge to the Indian way of thinking and living was a challenge to all Indian people. The great oneness of Oklahoma Indian tribes is spiritual. The unity—plains, woodland, prairie—is not so readily apparent in material life and culture but emerges clearly at a philosophical and spiritual level. Peoples as seemingly diverse as the Cheyennes and the Cherokees reflect Indian attitudes in their perception of the earth, the supernatural, and the association of man's spirit and the spirits of animals.[74]

The Cheyenne Wolf Soldiers, the last of the seven great Cheyenne soldier societies to be organized, served as a defensive and protective association. The Cheyenne soldier-society warrior, draped in the skin of a wolf, sought protective power and acquired strength from the animal. Richard West, the Cheyenne artist, has captured this animal warrior as lawman in his paintings and sculptures of the Wolf Soldier.[75] The Cherokees too had many wolf songs and medicine formulas as well as customs and legends about the wolf. Even after the Cherokees had adopted their highly acclaimed Anglo-based laws and constitution and established peace officers or light-horsemen modeled after frontier sheriffs, they turned to the animal powers of the spirit world. In the 1960s, Jack and Anna Kilpatrick came upon the following ritualistic formula calling upon the spirit of the wolves to aid and protect Cherokee peace officers:

> Now! Little Wolves! Very quickly all of you bark
> so that nothing can climb over.
> They cross your Path at the treetops.
> Now! Big Wolves! They just come trailing you.
> Now! "They will corner you right now in the
> Wolf places," I will be saying![76]

This spiritual man-animal relationship is described by Barry Holstun Lopez in his highly acclaimed study *Of Wolves and Men* (1978). "It is hard for the Western mind to grasp," he explains, "and take seriously the notion that an Indian at times could *be* wolf, could actually participate in the animal's spirit, but this is what happened. It wasn't being *like* a wolf; it was having the mind set: Wolf."[77]

Despite such shared values and perspectives Oklahoma's tribes were often hostile, either at war with each other or, at least, regularly engaged in skirmishes among themselves. For example, the Osages and the Cherokees fought intermittently for much of the first quarter of the nineteenth century. Upon many occasions, such as the spring of 1829, large tribal groups of Oklahoma Indians united to raid hostile Indians from across the Texas border.[78] Oklahoma tribes often attempted to unite and work together to resolve their mutual difficulties through "international councils" held in the Indian Territory. In June 1843 several thousand tribesmen from eighteen tribes met for four weeks to seek the common end of "improvement and security" and "a better understanding of the changes taking place about them." Eight interpreters were required to translate the eloquent speeches and great debates which resulted in agreements such as a pact on extradition of prisoners from other tribal territories.[79]

The continued military presence at Oklahoma forts provides evidence of frontier conflicts and of the threats to Indian safety from border ruffians, other tribes, and internal tribal wars.[80] Warring elements in Plains tribes raided back and forth across the border areas, taking white and Mexican captives and pursuing what Indians called "war—the beloved occupation." The Kiowa calendar records dozens of skirmishes and raids. It noted in 1837, "Cheyennes massacred on upper Red River"; in 1838–39, "Battle with Arapahoes"; in

1841, "Pawnee massacred on the South Canadian"; in 1852, "Allied tribes defeated by Pawnees"; in 1855–56, "Raid into Mexico"; in 1856–57, "Tipis seized by Cheyennes"; and in 1858–59, "Expedition against the Utes."[81]

No Indian war was more difficult for United States policy makers or more brutal for the participants than an Indian civil war such as the Cherokee conflict that followed the Trail of Tears. The brutal assassinations of Major Ridge, Elias Boudinot, and John Ridge emasculated the leadership of the anti-Ross Cherokees and launched a bloody guerrilla war that lasted from 1839 until at least 1846 and erupted again in the factionalism of the American Civil War.[82] Oklahoma Indian tribes allied with both the North and the South, with some tribes such as the Creeks bitterly divided and at war among themselves. When the Cherokee leader Stand Watie became the last Confederate general to surrender, the Indian Territory lay in devastation. It was a burnt-over land, a minor battlefield in a white man's war, destined to become a major target for the white man's postwar expansionist dreams.[83]

That early autumn before the American Civil War is the time about which Indians still dream. That haunting period seems to send forth the ghosts of Oklahoma's aboriginal spirit. Lynn Riggs, the Indian playwright, brought back a ghost warrior in *The Cherokee Night* (1936).[84] Returning from a victorious 1817 battle, the spirit speaks to a group of Indian mixed breeds picnicking one hundred years later on Osage Chief Claremont's Mount. The spirit warrior dressed in traditional regalia proclaims "this is the way we were meant to be . . . in our full pride, our last glory." The old Indian conjures up this historic past and asks these Indian descendants, "Have you forgot?" And as if to remind those who might never have known, he recreates the glories of his own age and of the freedom of the Indian nationhood.

> Have you forgot the use of the tomahawk and the bow?
>
> Not only in war — in quiet times — the way we lived:
>
> Have you forgot the smoke fire, the well-filled bowl?
> Do you speak with the River God, the Long Person no more —
> no more the vast Horned snake, the Giant Terrapin,
> with Nuta, the Sun?

Indian resting. Courtesy of the Oklahoma Historical Society.

Indian historians at work. Comanche and Kiowas painting their tribal stories on a buffalo robe, ca. 1875. Courtesy of the Oklahoma Historical Society.

A white watches an Indian painting the story of a great battle. Indians on horseback fight bearded white men who have come with guns to drive the game from their lands. Courtesy of the Oklahoma Historical Society.

War and Rumors of War, by Creek-Cherokee artist Joan Hill. A council of elders is gathered in this modern Indian painting. Courtesy of the Philbrook Art Center, Tulsa.

Indian Stalker, by Kiowa artist Stephen Mopope. The quiet quest of the Plains hunter is a haunting memory and a familiar theme in Oklahoma Indian paintings, as in this work by Mopope, one of the "Five Kiowas." Courtesy of a private collector.

Peace Pipe Prayer to the Spirit, silkscreen by Potawatomi Woody Crumbo. The smoke, the cedar, the fire, the buffalo, the pipe, and the feather are used by the Indian spiritualist. Courtesy of the McFarlin Library, University of Tulsa.

Cheyenne Wolf Warrior, painting and wood sculpture by Cheyenne artist Richard West. Members of this police and peace-soldier society of the Cheyennes drape themselves in the skins of wolves and thereby acquire the animal's power and spirit. Courtesy of a private collector.

Indian Sun Dance, by Richard West, a painting of the third day of a Cheyenne dance. This summer celebration was central to Oklahoma's Plains Indian culture. Courtesy of the Philbrook Art Center.

Indian with Horse, by Buffalo Meat, an early Cheyenne artist. He captures his tribe as they were caught mid-culture in the closing days of the nineteenth century. Courtesy of the Oklahoma Historical Society.

Osage protest drawing, a scratch-board illustration from a formal written protest by the Osages against the establishment of a territorial government and the coming of the railroads. Courtesy of the Shleppey Collection, University of Tulsa.

Chapter 2
THE DARK WINTER OF
SETTLEMENT AND STATEHOOD

The close of the American Civil War and the 1867 Indian treaty gathering at Medicine Lodge in Kansas signaled the beginning of the end of the old, free Indian nationhood. New treaties forced upon the Five Civilized Tribes at Fort Smith in 1866 contained provisions that ultimately opened the way for railroads to cross their domains and for the white onslaught that followed.[1] The signing of the Treaty of Medicine Lodge with leaders of Plains tribes, including the Kiowas, the Cheyennes, the Arapahos, and the Comanches, foreshadowed the federal government's effort to confine the tribes to reservations and compel them to follow the "white man's road."[2]

The Indian understood the dangers of the railroad, the white farmer, and the settler's wanderlust. In the more than forty years from the Civil War to Oklahoma statehood in 1907 the Indian became the victim of what Stephen Vincent Benét called "the American disease":

> Americans are always moving on.
> It's an old Spanish custom gone astray.
> A sort of English fever, I believe,
> Or just a mere desire to take French leave. . . .[3]

The Comanche Chief Ten Bears had foreseen the inevitable consequences of white settlement in his response to the military threats at the Treaty Council of Medicine Lodge. Ten Bears gave four thousand of his fellow Indians a frightening glimpse of what the coming decades would bring:

> There are things which you have said to me which I do not like. They were not sweet like sugar, but bitter like gourds. You said that you wanted to put us upon a

reservation, to build us houses and make us medicine lodges. I do not want them. I was born upon the prairie where the wind blew free and there was nothing to break the light of the sun. I was born where there were no enclosures and where everything drew a free breath. I want to die there and not within walls. . . . I lived like my fathers before me, and like them, I lived happily. . . . The white man has the country which we loved, and we only wish to wander on the prairies until we die.[4]

The Oklahoma Indian was caught on the crest of one of those great cycles that recur throughout American history. Westward expansion was itself an old story. Many of the Indians removed to Oklahoma, including the Shawnees, the Cherokees, the Senecas, and the Creeks, had been caught in earlier stages of the cycle. But this expansion was somehow different. It was more determined, better organized, and much faster, more efficient, and more difficult to resist. Powered not only by technological marvels such as the railroads, the steam engine, the mechanical harvester, the new expansion was also propelled by the "go-getter" spirit that infused the nation after the war. The military energy of the Union victory survived on the frontier. A determination to thrust the nation westward ruled in Congress and, more important, in the boardrooms, taverns, and churches. Landless Americans from older sections and newer emigrants who had temporarily settled elsewhere demanded Indian lands. There was no place left to remove the Indian, and there was little sympathy for the preservation of a way of life that left farmlands unturned, coal unmined, and timber uncut.

The old Indian hunter way and the new white industrial way could not coexist. Even the Five Civilized Tribes who had borrowed from the Anglo-Americans were, in their own way, too Indian. All their tribal lands were owned in common by the members of the tribes, and much of their land lay fallow. The Five Tribes were especially vulnerable because they had organized as agrarian societies and thus the white man more easily saw their domain as "surplus agricultural lands." Equally disturbing to the white entrepreneur, commercial exploitation of the Five Tribes' timber and mineral resources was restricted by the tribal laws. Indian rights—both economic and political—were jealously guarded. Economic preferences shown to tribal citizens were resented by whites who wanted to convert the riches of Indian land into gold and greenbacks. Furthermore, portions of these agricultural lands were leased to cattlemen or used by Indians who were themselves cattle barons. The Plains Indian's roaming hunter culture with the seasonal migration patterns following the herds was marked for extinction on both economic

32

and moral grounds. The goals and values of white and Indian civilization were incompatible.

The Indian understood what was happening and protested loudly and often. In 1874 chiefs and leaders of the Osage Nation met at Bird Creek and issued a "protest against the establishment by Congress of a Territorial Government of the United States, over the Indian Nations." A drawing, reproduced below the signatures of such revered Osage chiefs as Black Dog, White Hair, Jim Bigheart, and Young Claremont, expressed the fears of all the Indians of Oklahoma. The primitive sketch, entitled "Indian Territory," showed a train engine of the "No Soul Railroad" running over the body of an Indian caught on the iron track. The inscription was "Proposed End," with an arrow pointing to the body of the Indian. At the very bottom were the words: "23,000,000 acres to the railroads."[5] This tragic little drawing captures, in an almost prophetic way, the future of the Oklahoma Indian. Almost a decade earlier Roman Nose had voiced the same fears. "We will not have the wagons which make a noise [steam engines] in the hunting ground of the buffalo. If the palefaces come farther into our land, there will be scalps of your brethren in the wigwams of the Cheyenne," the great Chief warned.[6]

By 1889 the life of the Oklahoma Indian was changing. The military balance of power rested with the white man. The great romantic, free, nomadic-hunter civilization of the plains was past or, at least, passing. The Plains Indian wars were coming to an end, with many Oklahoma tribal leaders held captive in distant jails. The brutal massacre known as the Battle of the Washita (1868), in which George Armstrong Custer attacked Black Kettle's peaceful Cheyenne village, demonstrated the growing disparity between the Indian "Spartans of the plains" and the white warriors. The "blue coats" appear more frequently and grow larger and larger in the Indian's own ledger-book drawings.[7] Even the golden days of intense tribal creativity were ending for the Five Civilized Tribes, who were now left fiercely struggling to preserve whatever steps toward acculturation they had earlier made.

The year 1889 might appear on an Oklahoma Indian calendar as "the time when white farmers came with wives." Oklahoma Indian tribes in a real sense were still sovereign—"domestic dependent nations," in the words of Chief Justice John Marshall. Until that fateful year, although subject to many federal regulations, Indians owned all the lands that were to become Oklahoma. Whites within their domain were there on Indian sufferance or were government or military officials. Illegal intruders were subject to expulsion under existing treaties. These sovereign Indian nations were the only groups in Oklahoma whose political power and landed estate would diminish with the establishment of territorial government that had begun in 1889 and culminated in the admission of Oklahoma to statehood in 1907.

A great drama opened Oklahoma's Indian lands and ended the exclusive Indian possession of these domains. Fifty thousand potential homesteaders vied to stake out claims to the ten thousand farms of 160 acres each. It was an epic if condensed enactment of the entire frontier-settlement process. The Oklahoma land rush of April 22, 1889, has been recreated in song and story, in novel and in film, but how the Oklahoma Indian came to that year of 1889 and what happened subsequently has been largely ignored.

Before 1889, when the United States acquired the disputed Unassigned Lands from the Creeks and Seminoles, Oklahoma was exclusively Indian country in a legal, political, and social sense. Not so after that eventful year 1889, when the first of a series of runs opened these tribal lands to white settlement (see map 3). By 1975 the Bureau of Indian Affairs reported that Oklahoma Indian tribal lands encompassed only 65,000 acres and that Indians as private citizens owned only a million acres.[8] The size of tribal acreage grows slowly from year to year but is still a fraction of the once great Indian empires.

The story of the dissolution of the Oklahoma Indian nations is primarily one of white policy and white power. By 1865, Indian tribes had begun to lose whatever hint of equality they may have once possessed. Indians were left primarily to react to the initiatives of white policy. By 1871 the treaty era had formally ended, and even the pretense of a negotiated equality had been replaced by the terrorizing potential of executive order and congressional governance.

The history of Oklahoma Indian and white relations is a conflicting story because there has never been a single, clearly articulated American Indian policy. The shifting American Indian policies always reflected the current white definition of the so-called Indian problem. Between 1776 and 1876 there were at least a dozen varied "solutions." When the Indian problem was seen by federal officials as one of "civilizing" the Indian, the "agents of civilization" were sent to teach the Indian to plant and spin. When it was seen to require a military subjugation of hostile tribes, the Indian administration was centered in the War Department. When it was a question of the salvation of souls, denominational Christianity was given funds to manage portions of Indian policy. And each new set of problems, revisions of policies, systems of regulations, and programs for sub-jugation inherited a layer of bureaucracy and a set of obligations and procedures from the previous ones. Furthermore, a great many internally inconsistent Indian policies were pursued simultaneously by the same agencies. In Indian issues the gap between articulated policy and actual implementation was always wide.[9]

Analysis of nineteenth-century white policy toward Oklahoma Indians is confused because Indian-white relations cannot be under-stood without consideration of the varied interests, goals, and re-sources of the parties involved. Indians and whites are not inter-changeable historical personages. The whites—the Christian mis-sionary, the French hunter, the Union soldier, the illegal intruder on Indian lands, the '89er settled on her farm, the intermarried white merchant, the woman touring for the Indian Rights Association, the attorney for the allotment and sale of Indian lands, the deputy sheriff from the court at Fort Smith, and the Quaker agent—played different roles in the ultimate opening of Oklahoma Indian lands to white settlement. Indians within the same tribe had differing interests, goals, and values. For example, significant numbers of Indians cooperated with corporate and railroad interests to open the state to commercial development.[10] Furthermore, a distinction must be made between the relations of individual white citizens with individual Indian people and the government-to-government relations of the United States with Indian tribal units. The government often dealt or attempted to deal with single Indians, splinter groups, disgruntled factions, and unrecognized tribal "spokesmen." Indian and white roles might over-lap or conflict, as in the case of an intermarried Indian agent who was a land speculator or a mixed-blood tribal chief who had con-tracted as agent for tribal removal.[11]

Several sets of sometimes conflicting, often complementary goals are reflected in the policies that so dramatically changed the Okla-homa Indian country in the period from 1865 to 1907. Often treated as a single phenomenon, these practices and policies involved many separate tasks necessary to transform an Indian Territory owned exclusively by Indian tribal units into a state with land widely distrib-uted among non-Indian peoples. The fulfillment of these interrelated tasks fell heavily upon the Oklahoma Indian. First, the white needed to substitute a new way of life for the older Indian way. Further, land that was exclusively Indian-owned had to be taken out of common tribal ownership and shifted to new settlers and to individual Indian ownership. At the same time a new economic focus had to be created. Shifting the government unit from an individual Indian tribe to a white territorial force was an intermediate task. Finally, the Oklahoma Territory and the commonwealths of eastern Indian tribes had to be forged into a state. Thus from the Indian side we are dealing both with acculturation, or change of Indian culture, and with allotment, or distribution of Indian lands. These goals became the twin cornerstones of assorted nineteenth-century Indian reform policies, including the Dawes Act. Because white settlement, Indian land allotment, and the attempted cultural transformation occurred in Oklahoma at approximately the same time, it is difficult to deal with each in isolation. Taken together, these tasks dominated the life of Oklahoma Indians into the twentieth century.

In 1887, when the Dawes Act provided for allotting tribal lands to individual Indians, the American Indians' heritage in land totaled 138 million acres. Less than fifty years later, when the allotment policy was abandoned, only 48 million acres were left in Indian hands. Even more dramatic was the almost total collapse of the Oklahoma Indians' tribal holdings. Before allotment at the turn of the century the entire Indian Territory of 20 million acres in eastern Oklahoma was the exclusive property of self-governing tribal entities, primarily the Cherokees, the Creeks, the Choctaws, the Chickasaws, and the Seminoles. Today virtually the entire acreage of this rich domain of prosperous agricultural and mineral lands has passed from Indian hands. At the turn of the century "there was not a pauper Indian amongst them."[12] Today, three-quarters of a century later, the heartlands of these once-powerful tribes are filled with unemployment and destitution. The Oklahoma Indian settlement areas are primary battlegrounds for any war on poverty.[13]

How did this happen? How was the entire Indian Territory, a maturing political entity at one time destined to become the Indian state of Sequoyah, so quickly transferred from Indian to white hands? What transformed many of these Indian people from proud, prosperous, self-reliant citizens of their own small republics into landless, manipulated outcasts in a white state? The conventional wisdom is that these Indians suffered at the hands of mighty enemies—land-hungry railroad barons and zealous land developers—who were able to translate evil designs into Indian policy with bribes and six-shooter diplomacy.

There is some truth in these old myths, but the most disastrous policies for the tribes of the old Indian Territory were not the exclusive product of frontier villains. They were also created, supported, and ultimately adopted by liberal, pro-Indian Christian reformers. The "good works" of the Indians' friends created conditions ripe for the "evil deeds" of the Indians' exploiters. Over the years the Indians' friends have been particularly troublesome to Oklahoma's native people. A self-proclaimed purity of heart has not automatically guaranteed wisdom of policy. Many kind souls with the most benevolent purposes have produced Indian laws with malevolent results.

The white advocates of reform policy, the Indians' friends, were determined to make little red Farmer Joneses and native Old MacDonalds out of the American Indians. The Oklahoma Indian was to become another lost race in the American melting pot. He was to abandon his tribal lands, own his own farm, and compete for material goods. Two stages of development were thus required. Oklahoma's Plains Indians and other nomadic tribes had to be settled on a fixed reservation, since only then could tribal lands be assigned to individuals. Surplus lands would then become available for white settlement, with allotted lands available for later purchase by whites. To accomplish all this called for a government-supervised division of the commonly owned and held tribal lands among the individual members of the tribes. Implicit in this program was the assumption that this was the Christian God's plan and man's reward. These programs did not work. They robbed the Indian not only of his land but also of much that was working in his own traditional culture. The Oklahoma Indian was asked to sacrifice many of the best parts of his culture for most of the worst parts of the white culture.[14]

The long-range result of federal policy was that by the time of statehood in 1907 many Oklahoma Indians were handed land with a negotiable title. It was a fee simple absolute title in many cases and subject only to a limitation or restriction by supervision for a term of years in other cases. Thus most Oklahoma Indians were destined to become landless, because Indian tribes no longer held the land, and title soon passed to whites. Thus was lost Indian land, allotted over the protests of the vast majority of Indians who wished to retain tribal ownership.

The process of transforming Indian culture into white proved more difficult than substituting the name of a white settler or speculator for the Indian name on allotted land deeds. It was relatively easy to put names to paper and to divide up the real estate, but the cultural resilience of the American Indian amazed even the most dedicated reformer. "Indian renaming" was perhaps the most symbolically significant attack on the Oklahoma red man. Officials under the direction of the commissioner of Indian Affairs simply changed the names of Indian people, selecting new ones or reversing their old ones because of "silly or disgusting translations" of Indian proper names. The effort reached a climax in 1903 among Oklahoma's Southern Cheyenne. The Indians complained that they did not recognize the translations and refused to use the new white names. Hamlin Garland, though a strong supporter of the policy, wondered whether "the ones working on the rolls are not revising from the white man's point of view with a feeling that the names ought to be as nearly Anglo as possible. My notion is to treat them as we would Polish or Russian names— *retain as much of the Cheyenne as we can easily pronounce* and above all secure the pleased co-operation of the red people themselves."[15]

Most attacks on Indian civilization were not as subtle as the renaming programs. Indian agents were ordered to use the full force of the law to achieve assimilation. To the Indian and the agent this battle was to the death. Commissioner Hiram Price proclaimed that "one of two things must eventually take place, to wit, either civilization or extermination of the Indian. Savage and civilized life cannot live and prosper on the same ground. One of the two must die."[16] Photographs from this era capture the Indian as a people whose lifeway was disintegrating. Their traditional culture was drawing to an end, not because the Indian had changed or wished to change but because the white had determined to change the Indian. The Oklahoma Indian was the most conspicuous victim of federal policies of the middle to late nineteenth century. Those policies outlawed almost all conduct that was traditionally Indian and sought to substitute conduct that was decidedly white. The reports to the Indian commissioners in the year 1889 describe those policies in the context of Oklahoma's Indian tribes.

The Indian agent as administrator of federal policy played a major role in the effort to modify Indian life especially among the Plains Indians. Oklahoma Indian agents changed with increasing regularity and functioned with varying degrees of dedication, concern, and honesty. Charles Ashley, of the Cheyenne-Arapaho Agency, complained that insufficient clerical help "made it impracticable . . . to visit the Indians at their homes and the different farming districts," which "preclude[d] the possibility of my making any report based on personal knowledge of these Indians."[17]

Anyone who has dealt with a government bureaucracy will sympathize with E. C. Osborne, the agent at the Ponca, Pawnee, Oto, and Tonkawa Agency. He complained to the commissioner:

When I attempt to explain some of the vicissitudes of the life of an Indian agent, it will be clearly seen that it tries the nerves, patience, and pride of one to hold the position, and often he goes reeling through the duties imposed with wounded pride and shattered nerves, caused by some not-to-be-avoided obstacle, while upon the other hand he is being strangled to death by necessary "red tape" or "criminal propositions."[18]

The frustration of the Indian and the Indian agent is illustrated by a conflict between the military and the Cheyennes and Arapahos over sanitation on the North Fork of the Canadian River near Fort Reno. The military built a sewage system near Darlington "[that discharged] its filth into the river about 1½ miles above the point where water is taken for agency and school use." Agent Ashley complained of this military indifference to the health of the Indians of his agency:

A little more piping would have carried it below the point at which water is taken for the agency and school. . . . The low state of the river at this season of the year renders the water totally unfit for use. The source of water supply for the agency will have to be abandoned if an epidemic of typhoid fever is to be avoided.[19]

Indians who viewed themselves as independent peoples were not always cooperative. Even though they might no longer have the military force to defeat the white man, Indians had subtle ways to slow the agents and their bureaucracy. The extent to which the territorial Indians perceived themselves as sovereign is reflected in the story of Little Raven, a Cheyenne-Arapaho chief, who with great statesmanship and Indian humor objected to the house the government proposed to build for him near Darlington. Little Raven had been to Washington and Philadelphia and had met with the president at the White House. "The house of the Great White Father was big and fine," Little Raven told the agent. Since he was one of the principal chiefs of the Arapahos, as the president was the principal chief of the white people, would the agent see that his house was built like the White House in Washington? When the agent told Little Raven that it would cost too much money, the chief answered with an argument that modern-day government officials seem to have adopted. Little Raven explained that he knew that money was made in Washington because he had been taken to the mint to see it. Would the agent send word to the mint to make enough money to build him a house like the president's? The agent compromised and gave Little Raven one of the government buildings at Cantonment for his house, but the chief "kept a tipi in his yard, and when he longed for the old ways that were passing, he could stay there."[20]

"I find from four years of experience," the Ponca agent reported, "that to substitute the ways of the white man for the ways of the Indian cannot be achieved short of a prolonged, very painstaking, and very patient work" because "small faith in the advice or counsel of the white man remains with the Indian character of today."[21] A more optimistic attitude prevailed on the Cheyenne-Arapaho Reservation, where the agent wrote the commissioner that "results are what instill confidence in an Indian, and he is not slow in availing himself of anything that he is convinced . . . is beneficial."[22]

"The cow road," Carl Sweezy wrote, "was different from the buffalo road in more ways than anyone, white or Indian, had realized, and the old people could not learn it in a hurry." This Arapaho artist recalled that white people like "Alfalfa Bill" Murray had gone to Mexico or South America to take up a "new road of their own" and when they failed had "come back to their old homes to start over again." But, as he noted, "we had no home to go back to; we could only follow the old road as long as it lasted, while we learned the direction of the new one."[23]

The new direction—the corn road—was for the Indian a very different one. The Arapahos, Sweezy explained, had always

lived in bands, with their tipis side by side, their horses grazing together, and with hunting and fighting and worship all carried on by the group. It took years to learn to settle down on a farm and work alone and see one's neighbors only once in a while. Neither we nor our dogs nor our ponies understood this new way of white people. To us it seemed unsociable and lonely, and not the way people were meant to live.[24]

To assure that white values lived and Indian civilization died, the federal government used the full power of the law. They established "courts of Indian offenses," the goal of which was to eliminate "heathenish practices." As Secretary of the Interior Henry M. Teller noted in 1883, one of the major criminal offenses to be wiped out was the "continuance of the old heathenish practices of dances such as the sun dance, scalp dance, etc." Teller argued that at such dances "the audience assents approvingly to [the Indians'] boasts of falsehood and the young listener is informed that this and this only is the road to fame and renown. The result is the demoralization of the young, who are incited to emulate the wicked conduct of their elders."[25]

The thrust of this federal criminal law was to end Indian culture. That is reflected in the text of the "Rules for Indian Court," which defined offenses as follows:

> *Dances, etc.*—Any Indian who shall engage in the sun dance, scalp dance, or war dance, or any other similar feast, so-called, shall be deemed guilty of an offense. . . .
>
> *Practices of Medicine Men*—Any Indian who shall engage in the practices of so-called medicine men, or who shall resort to any artifice or device to keep the Indians of the reservation from adopting and following civilized habits and pursuits, or shall adopt any means to prevent the attendance of children at school, or shall use any arts of a conjurer to prevent Indians from abandoning their barbarous rites and customs, shall be deemed to be guilty of an offense. . . .
>
> *Misdemeanors*—And provided further, that if an Indian refuses or neglects to adopt habits of industry or to engage in civilized pursuits or employments, but habitually spends his time in idleness and loafing, he shall be deemed a vagrant and guilty of a misdemeanor.[26]

To the Indian this new life was discouraging, demeaning, and debilitating. Health problems among the Oklahoma Indians were serious, particularly among the upper woodland Indians and former nomadic families confined on permanent reserves. The 1889 report of the Osage Agency noted that "year by year their numbers decrease, the mortality being largely among the children."[27] In 1876 more than 2,000 Pawnees were removed to the Oklahoma reservation. The agent reported, "There has been a yearly decimation, and now they number only 851, being a loss of 1,375 in thirteen years." The cultural viewpoint of the agent was clear in his conclusion: "This fearful loss is largely due to the existence of constitutional diseases, while the incorrigible medicine man adds his list to the deathroll."[28]

"I pray every day, and hoe onions."[29] Thus a young Kiowa named Koba, or the Wild Horse, described his life as a boarding-school student being educated to accept the "civilized" ways. The federal government viewed education as a primary force in destroying the old Indian ways. Not just the Plains Indians but Indians of all of Oklahoma's tribes had their lives revolutionized by the attempts of reeducation. Koba, an early Indian artist, may have sensed the transformation in more dramatic terms than other Indians of Oklahoma, but the magnitude of the change was apparent to all. The full brunt of the effort of reeducation was directed toward Indian children who were shipped away from the reservation or brought together at reservation schools. The philosophy was most simply expressed by the founder of Carlisle School: "Kill the Indian and save the man."[30]

Aged Indian men and women still remember the harshness of this foreign educational experience of their childhood. Indian children are by white standards indulged by their families. But at Indian boarding school the youngsters were forbidden to speak their native tongues and were punished—often beaten—if they lapsed into their own languages. The directives issued in 1887 by the commissioner of Indian Affairs continued long after Oklahoma statehood: Indian children must speak English. "The language which is good enough for a white man or a black man ought to be good enough for the red man. It is also believed that teaching an Indian youth in his own barbarous dialect is a positive detriment to him."[31] A strange stiffness, a discordant image shows forth from the photographs of Indian youths at school: whether standing over washboards doing laundry or in the kitchen baking pies, the boys and girls seem to be indulging their white teachers in what they consider a great and absurd game of playing at white man.

While education was directed at Indian children, occupational reform was a program for adults, and the primary area of that reform was agricultural. The Indian male was to earn his living as a farmer, working the fields with horse and plow. Not only cultural resistance but bureaucratic failures doomed any hope of success of the plans to make Indian farmers of the warrior-plainsmen. At the Kiowa, Comanche, and Wichita Agency the report of 1889 notes: "Our seed oats arrived so late that a failure in the crop could be predicted with a certainty before they were planted."[32] Planting was made difficult because Indian ponies were clearly inappropriate as plow horses. Agent Myers wrote the commissioner recommending that

at least 1,500 acres of land be broken for these Indians in the early spring, for the reason that their pony teams are too small and light for the work, and many of them have become discouraged about farming, as they have been unable to secure any help from the Government in this direction for two years past.[33]

Farming was foreign to the Plains Indian tradition. And yet some Indians became farmers. As N. Scott Momaday recalls in *Names,*

"The Kiowas never had an agrarian tradition, and indeed they were disdainful of their neighbors the Wichitas, Creeks, and Osages, who were planters." But these Indians had to "contend with the matter of survival." Momaday's grandfather "had very little choice in the matter," since "under the allotment system he had too little land to raise cattle as a business, and the whites had long since begun to close in on all sides." And so this proud Kiowa started up the corn road: "While many of his kinsmen gave themselves up to self-pity and despair, he sowed cotton, wheat, melons, and beans."[34]

For a while Plains tribesmen were freighters, working as teamsters driving horse wagons to deliver goods in and out of the agencies. In 1889 the Kiowas, Comanches, and Wichitas transported more than 883,903 pounds of freight to the agency and delivered another 1,477,381 pounds to the Cheyenne-Arapaho Agency. Indians also shipped for white traders. At the height of the freighter trade, the Cheyennes and Arapahos operated more than 250 wagons.[35] The pay for hauling was not great, but, as Sweezy notes, "we needed less then . . . and besides, we weren't freighting just for the pay we got, but for some of the kind of satisfaction that we once got out of hunting and fighting."[36]

The principal task of the Indian in the new Oklahoma was to find a way of sustaining the family, of keeping the body and the spirit alive. The problems were the same over the entire Indian country. As the Indian land was allotted, even the old farming ways of the Five Civilized Tribes could not be sustained. The testimony of a Cherokee before a Senate committee in 1906 summarizes the condition of members of a tribe that is generally regarded as one of the most affluent:

Before this allotment scheme was put in effect in the Cherokee Nation we were a prosperous people. We had farms. Every Indian in this nation that needed one and felt that he needed one had it. Orchards and gardens—everything that promoted the comforts of private life was ours, even as you—probably not so extensively—so far as we went, even as you in the States. Under our old Cherokee regime I spent the early days of my life on the farm up here of 300 acres, and arranged to be comfortable in my old age; but the allotment scheme came along and struck me during the crop season. What a condition! I have 60 acres of land left me; the balance is all gone. I am an old man, not able to follow the plow as I used to when a boy. What am I going to do with it? For the last few years, since I have had my allotment, I have gone out there on that farm day after day. I have used the ax, the hoe, the spade, the plow, hour for hour, until fatigue would throw me exhausted upon the ground. Next day I repeated the operation, and let me tell you, Senators, I have exerted all my ability, all industry, all my intelligence, if I have any, my will, my ambition, the love of my wife—all these agencies I have employed to make my living out of that 60 acres, and,

God be my judge, I have not been able to do it. I am not able to do it. I can't do it. And I am here to-day, a poor man upon the verge of starvation—my muscular energy gone, hope gone. I have nothing to charge my calamity to but the unwise legislation of Congress in reference to my Cherokee people. . . . I am in that fix, Senators; you will not forget now that when I use the word "I" I mean the whole Cherokee people. I am in that fix. What am I to do?[37]

In the eastern half of the state the Five Civilized Tribes were engaged in the same futile struggle to preserve the new "civilized Indian way" of life they had chosen to adopt. By 1889 the Creeks, Choctaws, Cherokees, Chickasaws, and Seminoles were a minority in their own land. "It would be difficult, if not impossible," Agent Leo Bennett speculated, "to find an equal population anywhere with greater diversity of nationality, education, occupation, and creed, and with fewer interests in common."[38] Of 177,000 people more than 120,000 were non-Indian. Indian Territory was overrun with illegal intruders. Bennett estimated that in 1889 there were 35,000 such persons in the Indian Territory. The Indian, or citizen population, of that territory, including full bloods, mixed bloods, adopted whites, and the former slaves totaled about 65,000. Little more than 50,000 of these were Indians by blood. Also present were an additional 45,000 white farm laborers and mechanics with their families, admitted under permits, and another 25,000 licensed traders, miners, railroaders, and government employees. More than 7,000 assorted claimants, sojourners, and visitors completed the total of 177,000.

Who were these intruding whites? How did they live? To Bennett they were "fugitives . . . outlaws of every class, murderers, thieves, whiskey peddlers, gamblers, prostitutes, etc." Their influence was "corrupting, their touch . . . polluting, and their example . . . demoralizing." Officials at the Union Agency agreed that "to their malevolent influence may be directly traced the extension of crime in this country."

Attitudes toward education illustrated the conflict between the Oklahoma Indian of the Five Tribes and the white intruder. "In no community," the Union agent wrote, "does the education of the young men and women receive greater encouragement than among the five tribes." In addition to the large number of mission schools each of the tribes operated its own national school system. The Choctaws had 170 common schools with 30 schools for their freedmen. The Cherokees operated 110 primary schools as well as their academies. The Cherokee male and female seminaries were sophisticated institutions of education, teaching such courses as advanced mathematics and Latin. The Chickasaws maintained similar school systems. The Creeks operated 36 day schools, and their land was the site of a number of important mission schools.

The contrast among the white children was disturbing. "Thousands of children of these intruding criminals are nurtured in crime," Bennett noted. "They are born in inequity and reared in unrighteousness and sin, without religion, without any restraining influence, and it does not cause any wonder that the child follows the footsteps of its parents."

The popular perception of Indian Territory at the close of the nineteenth century as a wild, lawless, last frontier was false. Isaac C. Parker, the famous "hanging judge," testified that

as to the lawless condition of Indian Territory . . . these are confined . . . to what I call criminal intruders. . . . During the twenty years I have been engaged in administering the law there, the contest has been one between civilization and savagery, the savagery being represented by the intruding criminal class. I have never found a time when the Indians have not been ready to stand by the courts in the carrying out of the law.

In fact, operation of law in the Indian country was cited as a model for the states because "the statistics . . . show there is better enforcement of criminal law in the Indian country, more men are arrested and convicted, than in any court in any state of this Union."[39]

The Indian police forces on the western reservations were also considered models of law enforcement. The agent for the Kiowas, Comanches, and Wichitas recommended increased pay for the Indian police officers because "the men comprising the force at this agency are honorable, truthful, and can be relied on to faithfully perform any duty assigned them."[40] In 1889 the Cheyenne-Arapaho agent reported "no record exists in the office of any crimes having been committed by the Indians during the past year." The Indian courts among the Plains tribes were important institutions in law enforcement, especially when a court was presided over by leaders such as the Kiowa Lone Wolf, the Comanche Quanah Parker, and Towaconie Jim. "Their decisions," the agent reported, "were generally fair, and always impartial, and are accepted with good grace by the Indians."[41]

In 1889 the Seminole Nation contained fewer than sixty whites, and Agent Bennett called it "the most peaceful and law-observing of the five nations," adding that "it is seldom that there is any clash in their affairs." The "absence of the Boomer" was the agent's explanation for "this peace and harmony."[42] Tragically, by 1898 the

Seminole Nation was the site of a flaring of mob violence that resulted in the burning deaths of two young Seminoles and the torture of others. Payment of indemnity was ultimately made to twenty-four members of the tribe.[43]

The federal government either would not or could not remove the army of illegal intruders from the Indian Territory. In 1889 the Union Agency removed only thirty intruders in the face of the Indians' demands that their treaty provisions required expulsion of these illegals. "It would require a regiment of soldiers to remove these persons and keep them out," federal officials replied. "Certain it is," they admitted, "that the Indian office has never been equal to the necessities in the case."

The misplaced faith of some Oklahoma Indian people is nowhere more obvious than in the 1889 Annual Message of Cherokee Chief Joel B. Mayes, which expressed faith that "the God of the white man is our God and has, in his mercy, been on the side of the Indian."[44] Mayes nonetheless recognized that

the same influences that drove the Cherokees from the ancient homes of their fore-fathers east of the Mississippi are beginning to marshal their forces and clamor for our land—you hear great, and what ought to be good, men and the great American Press, say "If we cannot buy it we will take it."

The United States government did force the Cherokees from their Outlet lands, and seven decades later the Indian Claims Commission found that this constituted an illegal taking for which the tribe was compensated.[45]

Other leaders of this era, such as the Comanche Quanah Parker (1845–1911), the Cherokee Redbird Smith (1850–1918), and the Creek Chitto Harjo (1846–1912?) still provide inspiration for Oklahoma's Indian people. Parker, the mixed-blood Comanche son of Cynthia Ann Parker, came to symbolize the Plains people. The great warrior established his bravery when he and a group of Comanches refused to accept the dictates of the Treaty of Medicine Lodge and battled to the end at Adobe Wells in Texas in 1874. Parker then led his people down the new road, became a famous tribal judge, and as a member in the Native American Church was a widely identified peyote figure. While willing to adjust to farming and the new economic ways, Parker continued to practice the old Comanche family way of having a number of wives. Ironically, while Parker remains to the present a controversial figure in his own tribe, the

Parker pattern of selective adaptation and resistance became the one Oklahoma's Indians generally followed.[46]

Another strand of Oklahoma Indianness is rooted in the tradition of Redbird Smith, in the traditionalist Cherokee Kee-Too-Wah, and in Chitto Harjo, the great leader of the traditionalist Creeks known as the Snakes. At the time of allotment Smith had protested to a group of United States Senators, showing them a copy of the Cherokee land patent and a feather given his great-grandfather at the treaty signing. "I will never change," he declared. "It extends to heaven, the great treaty . . . and is respected by the Creator, God." In the early 1900s, Chitto Harjo defied the federal courts and the United States Army in their effort to assign tribally owned lands to individual Creek citizens. The Creeks who opposed the allotment of Indian lands were accused of starting a white-promoted war known as the Crazy Snake Rebellion.[47]

The Creek poet Alexander Posey wrote a poem "On the Capture and Imprisonment of Crazy Snake, 1900" which expresses the spirit of Oklahoma's Indian resistance:

> Down with him! chain him! bind him fast!
>   Slam to the iron door and turn the key!
> The one true Creek, perhaps the last
>   To dare declare, "You have wronged me!"
> Defiant, stoical, silent,
>   Suffers imprisonment!
>
> Such coarse black hair! such eagle eye!
>   Such stately mien! — how arrow-straight!
> Such will! such courage to defy
>   The powerful makers of his fate!
> A traitor, outlaw, — what you will,
>   He is the noble red man still.
>
> Condemn him and his kind to shame!
> I bow to him, exalt his name![48]

Chitto Harjo was an eloquent man who spoke simply in his own defense: "At that time when we had these troubles it was to take my country away from me. I had no other troubles. I could live in peace with all else, but they wanted my country and I was in trouble defending it."[49]

The twin strands of the mixed-blood Parker and the full-blood Harjo are part of the great anomaly of the modern Oklahoma Indian.

The tenacity with which mixed bloods of an eighth or less Indian blood hold to the tradition is itself very Indian. It is part of the respect for what Ben Harjo, the Creek painter, has called "those who have gone before." This reflects the desire for continuity with a way of Oklahoma Indian life that may have had native roots in the state at least as early as 1808. Indianness has a tribal component that many whites do not understand. Before adoption of the white man's legal system the tribe controlled membership absolutely and prized it highly. Not a few Indians, including many mixed breeds, do not wish to be known as members of the white race, with the record they see of murder, forgery, and embezzlement.[50]

A strand of Oklahoma Indian self-help is illustrated by the action of the Quapaws in the allotment of their 56,000-acre reserve. In 1887 federal officials sought to provide each Quapaw with 80 acres of land, leaving a sizable surplus of tribal lands for sale to whites. The tribe protested; the federal government delayed action. The Quapaws then organized their own allotment program and under a resolution of the Quapaw Council in 1893 made allotments of 200 acres of land to each member of the tribe. The tribe kept all records and to finance the enrollment adopted into the tribe several white persons, who became known as "the fullblood white Quapaw." In 1895, Congress approved the acts of the Quapaw Council, and this tribe became the only one in history to carry out their own allotment program, having almost tripled the land that stayed in Indian hands.[51]

Among the Five Civilized Tribes the actual process of shifting tribal lands to individual members was accomplished with remarkable speed. The Dawes Commission's work of preparing the rolls began with the Curtis Act in June 1898 and continued through March 1907, with a few additional names being added in 1914.[52] In all 101,526 persons were placed on the final rolls of the Five Civilized Tribes. Full bloods constituted 26,794; another 3,534 were enrolled as having three-fourths or more Indian blood; 6,859 were listed as one-half to three-fourths Indian; 40,934 were listed as having less than one-half Indian blood. A separate roll of 23,405 blacks, known as freedmen, was prepared. Enrollments and land figures from the Dawes enrollment and allotment follow on page 49.

The total tribal land base was 19,525,966 acres, 15,794,400 acres of which were allotted. The balance of 4 million acres included 309 townsites, which were sold, and segregated coal and timber, as well as other unallotted lands, sold at public auction.

Tribe	Enrolled	Acres	Allotted
Cherokees	40,193	4,420,068	4,420,068
Creeks	18,712	3,079,095	2,993,920
Seminoles	3,119	365,852	359,697
Choctaws	26,730	6,953,048	8,091,386
Chickasaws	10,955	4,707,904	(jointly with Choctaws & Chickasaws)

Oklahoma Indians, especially full-blood descendants, suffer today from these earlier federal programs to enroll Indians in the Indian's own tribes and to allot to individual Indians their tribally owned domains. When the Dawes Commission rolls were drawn at the turn of the century, many traditionalist Indians like the Crazy Snake Creeks refused to enroll because they believed that the United States was violating its treaty promises. Many were enrolled against their will, but others escaped the roving enrollment parties. Thus Oklahoma's mixed-blood Indians are often federally recognized, while many full bloods and their descendants are treated as non-Indian. Other full bloods enrolled themselves as quarter-bloods or eighth-bloods so that they would not have restrictions on their lands and the need for guardians. As a result, in tribes such as the Choctaws, Seminoles, Cherokees, Creeks, and Chickasaws, whose rolls have been closed by act of Congress, descendants of these enrollees are denied educational and other Indian benefits to which, by their correct blood quantum, they are entitled.

The destruction of the governments and distribution of the lands of the Five Civilized Tribes were tragically ironic. These tribes had listened to Thomas Jefferson's advice about civilization and believed the white man when he said, "Follow my example and I will treat you as equal." The Indians' failure to survive as a political state was a white, not an Indian, failure. Again and again, as tribal accomplishments laid a foundation that would have preserved them as Indian peoples, the white man stepped in and destroyed the tribal accomplishments through legislation or force of arms. Brought to the Indian Territory at gunpoint in frozen winter over the Trail of Tears, one Creek remembered having been driven off "like wolves."[53] By the end of the nineteenth century the Indians had rebuilt their lives and civilization. They stood ready to accept admission to the

Union as the Indian state that would culminate their historic Jeffersonian compromise with the white man. Delegates from the eastern half of the state met in Muskogee in 1905 at the Sequoyah Convention to adopt a constitution and prepare the way for their new state. Instead of fulfilling the promises of eventual statehood, the United States government divided their tribal lands, abolished Indian courts, and ended their governing powers. Forced to abandon their dream of an Indian state of Sequoyah, they were merged into the state of Oklahoma.[54]

But the Indian and Indian attitudes were not so easily lost even in the statehood movement. Oklahoma may be the only state in which the Indian did have a significant and long-lasting impact on the form of state government and the nature of the constitutional legal system.[55] Many important Oklahoma constitutional provisions, such as prohibition of alien ownership of land and limitation on corporate buying or dealing in real estate, were products of the unique Oklahoma Indian experience. One group that predominated in the attitudes and development of the new Oklahoma government was the Five Civilized Tribes and the white citizens who allied with them to control the Oklahoma Constitutional Convention. Among the reasons for this influence was the experience gained in 1905 at the Sequoyah Constitutional Convention, a meeting called to prepare for the single statehood of the Indian Territory. William H. Murray held correctly that "some of the most important provisions of the [Oklahoma] Constitution derived their inspiration from the Sequoyah Constitution."[56]

Many regulations enacted by the Oklahoma Constitutional Convention represented a last desperate struggle not only of Indians and their nations but also of the small homestead farmers against what they, as Oklahomans, viewed as the chronic failures in other states. They were guarding against ills they had known: the foreign land barons of Texas, the octopuslike monopolies and trusts that dominated the oil resources of Kansas, and their own home-grown land-hungry real estate speculators and exploiters. The constitutional regulations that seemed so revolutionary and placed Oklahoma in the radical vanguard of state governments were products of this unique time and place. These provisions included the right granted to the state "to engage in any occupation or business for public purposes" (except agriculture), prohibition of monopolies, restrictions on "unlawful restraints of trade," control of banks and trust companies, prohibition of government aid to corporations, prohibition of alien ownership of land, and limitations on corporate buying, acquiring, or dealing in real estate.[57]

To understand the forces that bear upon these land-tenure and economic regulations, one must understand the state's Indian and settlement experience. Oklahoma was a vast territory only recently opened to white citizens and historically divided in such a way that it should never have been one state. The eastern half of the state was the old Indian Territory and had earlier sought statehood under its own banner as the Indian state of Sequoyah. Much of the western half of the state had belonged to the Plains Indian tribes but had been wrested from their control and, after a period of use through lease as cattle range, had been opened for small-farm homesteading with only a few scattered Indian areas remaining. "Single statehood" versus "double statehood" was widely debated in this area, which was popularly known as the Twin Territories. Oklahoma was formed by the symbolic wedding of the old Oklahoma and Indian territories.

By the time of Oklahoma statehood the Five Civilized Tribes had been operating their constitutional republics for more than three-quarters of a century. They were by no means novices at the white political process, but there was much that was Indian in their governments. Many of these aspects of Indianness were preserved in the outlook and attitudes of the state of Oklahoma. It is impossible to understand and appreciate Oklahoma life and government without an awareness of the absolutely unique experience of the government and operation of the Five Civilized Tribes. The leaders of the Indian republics became the leaders of the Sequoyah Convention, which in turn produced many of the leaders of the Oklahoma Constitutional Convention. The mark of Indian attitude in Oklahoma government goes far deeper than the Choctaw name Allen Wright suggested for the home of the red man.

In a way there was also something of the Indian-cattleman-farmer conflict present in Oklahoma's conception of law, land ownership, and the regulation of the state's resources. For before the opening of the western portion of the state to settlement by run, it had been "cow country," not "homes for farm folk," as latter-day state politicians liked to call it. Significant portions of Indian lands had been leased to white ranchers by or for the Indian tribes. Lands of both the Plains Indians and the Five Civilized Tribes were centers of cattle ranching. The historical clash over economic interests reflected in the opening of tribal lands to white settlement is portrayed by historian Edward Everett Dale, an eyewitness participant:

> When the great Indian reservations were opened to settlement it is popularly believed that the land was taken from the Indian and given to the white man. As a matter of fact the Indian did not use the land and so as an economic factor in the history of the region is negligible. The man who really used these lands was the ranch-man, and what really happened in the opening of large reservations to settlement was that the land was taken from the cattleman and given to the farmer, or its use changed by governmental action from grazing stock to the growing of crops. . . . The passing of the Indian reservation meant, largely speaking, the passing of the ranch cattle industry.[58]

By the time the Oklahoma Constitutional Convention met in Guthrie, the traditional Indian land-tenure system had been changed by government action. The Five Civilized Tribes had felt the sting of the Dawes Commission and the Curtis Act. Against their tribal protestations the vast lands formerly held in common had been distributed. The former tribal domain had been allotted, under federal law, on a per capita basis in fee simple to the individual members of the tribe subject to certain restrictions, including limitations on alienability. The process of allotting the lands of the great Oklahoma Indian Nations had set off a land grab of previously unequaled magnitude.[59]

Speculating in Indian land had led to the formation of land companies whose only purpose was to deal in this recently allotted land; wholesale abuse of the citizens of the Indian Nations was widespread. An understanding of this background clarifies some of the demand for the regulations in the Oklahoma Constitution preventing corporate ownership and speculation in real estate. Only large corporations and trusts, the delegates at Guthrie felt, could afford to acquire rights in land which, according to federal restrictions, would not become alienable, in many cases, for as long as twenty-five years.

Another concern long building among the Indian delegates and almost as important as the behavior of corporate land companies was railroad speculation in townsite development. The citizens of Indian Territory had found railroads concerned less with providing transportation than with securing rights in Indian tribal property. The lines were expert in the questionable practice of using the location of a railroad to promote their dubious land dealings, as well as generally exploiting mineral, timber, and agricultural resources. Railroad operations had long been a source of bitter internal strife in most of the tribes. Their leaders resented the way their own governments and tribal delegations in Washington had been abused by the railroad men and the government functionaries who danced to the tune of the railroad lobby. So railroads were corporations creating more than the usual fear of monopoly power; railroads had a record that many citizens of Indian Territory, including the president of the convention, William H. Murray, viewed as criminal.

A major concern that certainly motivated the Oklahoma Constitutional Convention was the protection of individual ownership of resources, especially the preservation and encouragement of individually owned and operated family farms. Equally certain is the fact that the number-one public enemy and primary corporate villain was perceived to be the Standard Oil Company. And one may further conclude that the regulation of agricultural and business monopolies was seen as a part of the same general issue. The problem seemed most critical at that point where the issues were overlapped by corporate combination of public transportation and access to agricultural and timber markets.

Thus a number of groups significantly influenced the development of constitutional attitudes in Oklahoma. Among these were the Indian tribes, especially the Five Civilized Tribes in the Indian Territory, the small farmer-settlers of the Oklahoma Territory, the cattlemen and ranchers, the infant but vigorous labor movement, and the powerful railroad interests and land-mineral speculators. The Oklahoma constitutional provisions regulating land and economic resources were produced by the interactions, clashes, and compromises between and among these powerful interests. To understand Oklahoma government one must remember that it was conceived when land speculators, Indians, cowboys, dirt farmers, and coal miners came together to settle on the laws that would control their own use of the resources of the new state.

"We spoiled the best territory in the world to make a state," Will Rogers joked. A white state like Oklahoma was inevitable, Rogers said, because "Indians were so cruel they were all killed by civilized white men for encroaching on white domain."[60] In 1907, while the constitutional convention was in session, Alexander Posey, the famed Creek poet, statesman, and satirist, wrote a series of letters from "Fus Fixico" in Indian dialect about the Indian reaction to statehood.

The Indians in Oklahoma

"Well, guess so," Tookpaka Micco say, "Alfalfa Bill and Boss Haskell was put near ready to let their work shine."

An' Hotgun he spit in the ashes an' say, "Well, so, not hardy."

An' Tookpaka Micco he say, "Well so what was trouble anyhow?"

An Hotgun he go on an' say, "Well, so they couldn't decide, what name to give the Great Spirit."

Then Tookpaka Micco, he smoke an' look under the bed an' say, "Well, so could settle their differences if they had recognized Confucius for Chinaman, an' Mohamet for the Turk, an' Saint Patrick for the Irishman, an' the almighty dollar for the American."[61]

Statehood was the bitter culmination of decades of conflict and of self-righteous programs to transform Indian Territory into a white commonwealth and make the American Indian into a red farmer. Few whites ever understood the depth of the Indians' agony at the passing of their nationhood. Dale, the dean of Oklahoma's white historians, wrote with some surprise of the sadness an Indian woman still felt when she remembered the 1907 festivities to celebrate Oklahoma statehood. This Cherokee woman, married to a white man, refused to attend the statehood ceremonies with her husband. He returned and said to her: "Well, Mary, we no longer live in the Cherokee Nation. All of us are now citizens of the state of Oklahoma." Tears came to her eyes thirty years later as she recalled that day. "It broke my heart. I went to bed and cried all night long. It seemed more than I could bear that the Cherokee Nation, my country and my people's country, was no more."[62]

Apache Indian camp, a village on the Oklahoma prairie in 1889, the year of the first land run. Courtesy of the Oklahoma Historical Society.

Tahlequah, capital of the Cherokee Nation, 1889. The tribe is gathered for the annual message of Chief Joel B. Mayes. Courtesy of the Worcester-Robertson Collection, University of Tulsa.

Lady Bountiful. Miss Roff, an Episcopal missionary, visiting a Plains Indian camp as part of the program to Christianize the "heathen savages." Courtesy of the Oklahoma Historical Society.

Wichita-Caddo Indians plowing. A major goal of white policy was to transform Indians from hunters into farmers. Courtesy of the Oklahoma Historical Society.

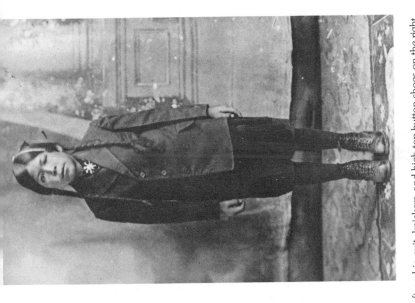

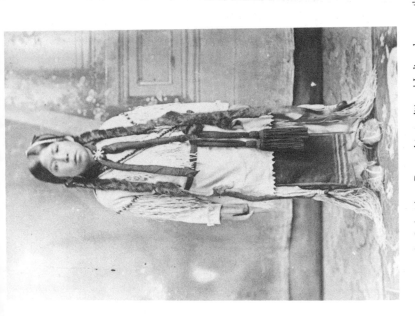

A Comanche Indian boy. Dressed in traditional Indian dress on the left and in suit, knickers, and higt-top button shoes on the right, the boy seems to be a before-and-after advertisement for acculturation. Courtesy of the Western History Collections, University of Oklahoma Library.

Indian dolls. A Christmas tree for Indian children and their families at the Episcopal Chapel, Anadarko, at the turn of the century. Courtesy of the Oklahoma Historical Society.

A class in session at the Riverside Indian School, 1901. Indian education was a cornerstone of the Indian reform movement. Courtesy of the Oklahoma Historical Society.

Indians working in a laundry at Riverside School to learn "good health" and a "trade," 1901. Courtesy of the Oklahoma Historical Society.

Indian girls at school: a Wyandot, a Seneca, and a Shawnee dressed in white attire. Courtesy of the Oklahoma Historical Society.

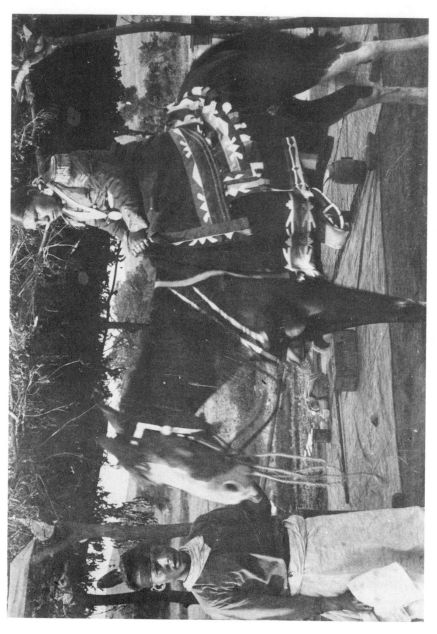

An Osage bride in wedding attire. Note the elaborate ribbon work on the skirt and the adaptation of the military coat. Courtesy of the Oklahoma Historical Society.

A rare photograph of a Ghost Dance in Oklahoma, ca. 1889, when the Ghost Dance movement and its search for a messiah and the return of the buffalo came to Oklahoma's Plains tribes. Courtesy of the Western History Collections, University of Oklahoma Library.

A Cheyenne-Arapaho village gathered for a Ghost Dance about two miles northwest of Fort Reno in August 1889. Courtesy of the Western History Collections, University of Oklahoma Library.

The last Sun Dance of the Poncas, ca. 1883. The federal government sought to end native ceremonial practices and specifically outlawed the Sun Dance. Courtesy of the Western History Collections, University of Oklahoma Library.

The Creek Ribbon Dance. Despite federal efforts to outlaw Indian celebrations, many traditional ceremonials such as this Creek women's dance are still important to Indian life. Courtesy of the Western History Collections, University of Oklahoma Library.

Chapter 3

THE LONG SPRING OF TRIBAL RENEWAL

Spring in Oklahoma can be as terrifying as it is unpredictable, as menacing as it is beautiful. Nobody, white or Indian, could have forecast at statehood the direction of Indian life in the coming years. At first it looked dark and gloomy. It seemed as if the winds of change might blow away even the sustaining visions left from that bright autumn of Indian nationhood. The changes statehood dealt to Oklahoma's Indians are mirrored in the changes to the old landscape itself. In 1930 an aged Kiowa, Eagle Plume, recalled the great prairie upon which he had grown old and contrasted it with the state high-ways over which he was now forced to ride:

The road and the plowing had changed the shape of the country. Where once it had run together and been an even, smooth, soft color, brown or green or red with the seasons, now there were edges to the colors, and they lay in sharp patterns. There were ditches beside the road that had never been there before, and with the change in the color and the shape of things, the feel of the world had changed.[1]

The drive to acculturate the Indian and the changing, urbanizing world of Oklahoma produced many who were uncertain and con-fused. Native responses such as the Ghost Dance and the peyote rituals were efforts to find a new but still Indian way to respond to the white world, just as Christianity held out yet another vision. The white world and the white value structure seized some Indians with the zealousness found in religious converts. The contrasts were great. Elsie Clews Parsons recorded a meeting with "an educated Indian" in 1927 in western Oklahoma.[2] "Incredibly great are the cultural differences today between the Kiowa generations," she noted. A Kiowa woman, Standing-Inside-Feathers, delighted in proclaiming how conservative she and her husband had remained: "He and me want to stay Indian, real Indian." Her son motored in one morning and spent two hours telling Parsons about the wealth and civilization of his Indian generation. Was there not, he asked, a girl living west of Hobart who owned $150,000 in oil land? Did he not himself own a home quite as good as any white man's?

John Joseph Mathews, the Osage writer, addressed the problem of Indian youth of transitional generations in his novel *Sundown* (1935).[3] Chal, his principal character, an Indian student attending a university soon after statehood, curses to himself, "I wish I didn't have a drop of God damn Indian blood in my veins." He "often wished he weren't so bronze" because "it set him off from other people." All this reflected what Mathews saw as the real-world conflict for the young Indian. In *Wah'Kon-Tah* (1932), Mathews recounted the reactions of an Osage who returned from the world of fast cars and hot music to the agency at Pawhuska:

The young man looked with pity upon his parents. He thought of how old-fashioned they were: his father still wearing his buckskin leggings and his beaverskin bandeau, his pale blue silk shirt and his blanket; his mother in her shirt, moccasins, and shrouding. They were certainly behind the times all right. No matter how swell he dressed he was always embarrassed thinking of his parents sitting out at the ranch. They couldn't even speak English. He wished he didn't have to speak Osage with them—it sure made him feel funny when they talked together in public at the Agency.[4]

Most Indians were not eager to abandon their heritage; rather, they were looking for something to sustain their Indianness. The Ghost Dance of the Paiute prophet Wovoka had been such a sustaining vision, with the promise that if the Indians practiced love, danced, and sang the songs, the millennium would come, the buffalo would return, and the souls of the departed would be with them. Even before statehood the Ghost Dance had burned itself out. It was not even the Battle of Wounded Knee (1890) in the Dakotas, where ghost dancers were massacred, that brought the vision to an end in Oklahoma. The dance could not bring back what was gone, and the depression of it all is reflected in the complete loss of hope in this Ghost Dance song:[5]

> My Father, have pity on me!
> I have nothing to eat.
> I am dying of thirst—
> Everything is gone.

A more lasting and sustaining way came to the Oklahoma Indian in the "Peyote Road," which the Comanches and Kiowas learned from the Mescalero Apaches in the 1870s and which was formally incorporated as the Native American Church in Oklahoma on October 10, 1918. Some believe that as many as a third of Oklahoma's cultural Indians other than the Five Tribes participate in peyotism. Involving the ritual use of the peyote button, the head of which has been sliced from the root and dried, the religion is a cultural reinforcement. The ways and rituals vary, but as in the Covering of Pipe Ceremony and the Sun Dance, there must always be a vow for something important to the individual, to the tribe, or to the world as a whole. The ritual items, such as the gourd rattles, fans, and drums, have often drawn attention from the songs and prayers. As Carl Sweezy observed of peyotism:

> When the service ends at sunrise, and the fast is broken . . . , those who have taken part face the day and the world before them with a new sense of beauty and hope and goodness in their hearts. Left Hand spoke the truth: There are many ways to God.[6]

Archie Blackowl, a Cheyenne descendant of Crow Necklace and Roman Nose, recalled the pride, agony, and cultural resilience of the Indian child taken against his will to the white schools:

> When I was about seven years old they took me to this damn Indian school of the government's and we all had to stand in line and they cut my hair off. They just cut my braids off and threw them into a box with all the other children's braids! My old grandmother went over there and got them. And they took all my homemade clothes away from me. My grandfolks stayed at the winter camp *all* winter to be near me. And when I got awful hungry I used to run down there and they'd feed me. It was hard being Indian in them days. Later I learned to be proud.[7]

Thomas Wildcat Alford, a Shawnee born before the Civil War who lived into the period of statehood, questioned the meaning of the Indian-white acculturation. "Our young people," he wrote in 1936, "are taking up the ways of the white people. Whether that will lead them to a higher civilization or to a more flagrant vaunting of their freedom, I do not know." The high-powered cars, the fashions, the drinking caused him to ask, "Is all this civilization?" Wildcat concluded his book with cautious optimism:

> In every human heart there is a deep spiritual hunger for an abiding, steadfast faith, a positive, satisfying belief. . . . My own sons and daughters are . . . going out into the tide, taking their places in the economic life of the country. I have tried to instill into their hearts and minds some of the principles of my people.[8]

The general condition of the Oklahoma Indian after statehood was severely distorted in the popular imagination by the great Osage oil boom.[9] In 1923 the Osages received $27 million in payment for petroleum leases and for the oil under their 1.5-million-acre reserve. Some years each Osage got more than $50,000 for each headright share of the mineral estate. Other tribes, such as the Quapaws had owned coal, lead, and zinc. Still other tribal members had oil in their individual allotments, but it belonged collectively to all Osages listed on the headrights roll.

The great Oklahoma oil industry rested on Indian lands. The Nellie Johnstone No. 1 and the Glenn Pool of Ida Glenn bear the names of the Indian allottees whose land was leased for drilling. Other names like that of Jackson Barnett (known as "the richest Indian in the world") have gone down in the legends of the petroleum industry to capture the spirit of a time when some Indian oil million-aires could be almost as extravagant as the white men who were pumping their lands dry.

The oil madness climaxed in the "Osage reign of terror." Sys-tematic murders of Osages, particularly the family of Lizzy Q, were planned to transfer vast fortunes to intermarried whites. Ernest Burkhart was jailed, but more than twenty murders were never solved. The great Osage chief Fred Lookout may have been right when he said: "My people are not happy. Some day this oil will go and there will be no more checks every few months from the great white father. There'll be no more fine motor cars and new clothes. Then I know my people will be happier."[10]

The Great Depression brought to the rest of the nation economic conditions that many Oklahoma Indians had known since statehood. In 1930 and 1931 the United States Senate held a series of hearings on reported famines among Oklahoma Indians.[11] Ross Daniels testi-fied that "they are in bad condition. A lot of them do not have bread and grease. They are in the worst sort of condition. I believe they have died from the effects of improper nourishment." S. W. Peak reported, "I have not found any family that was faring anyways like they ought to." And Jackson Wolfe predicted that "we are going to be turned out like hogs. We have not much land any more. It is pretty nearly all gone. The way it is going now we will be blowed up; that is all. We won't have any home or any place."

The process by which the Indian became landless is part of a dark chapter in white Oklahoma's relations with its Indian citizens. Millions of acres and other accumulated resources were wrested from the Indians.[12] Of the thirty million allotted acres more than twenty-seven million passed from Indians to whites. Among the more common devices used by their fellow Oklahomans were fraudulent deeds signed by others than the owners of the land; purchase prices far below market or actual appraised value of land; payments of bribes for court approval of fraudulent land sales; excessive administrative and guardianship fees; embezzlement of Indian money and personal expenditure of Indian trust funds; false heirship claims or destruction of Indian wills; and gifts to charities or individual citizens of Indian assets without the knowledge or approval of Indian or court.

Kidnapping, dynamiting, and murder were not uncommon devices to acquire land. Spectacular crimes occurred. An epidemic of deaths broke out among aged Indians. Just before the deaths real estate speculators bought wills from the Indians for small sums. In the midst of all this corruption many lawyers who ought to have been guarding the Indians, preserving the integrity of the judicial process, and policing the behavior of their colleagues were assisting the speculators. Other lawyers who were not participants stood by while their brothers at the bar took from full bloods allotments and major fortunes either by outright theft or through unwarranted or excessive charges for their services.[13] This is not an ennobling chapter in the history of Oklahoma's relations with Indian people. Knowing of this earlier chapter should help Oklahomans understand, at least in part, Indian hostility toward state government, lawyers, and the courts.

The heart of the New Deal Indian Program in Oklahoma was the Oklahoma Indian Welfare Act (1936) under which groups of enrolled tribal members could organize for their common welfare and secure a federal charter as local cooperative associations. Only eighteen comparatively small groups came under these provisions in the years between 1937 to 1942, although ultimately fifty-one tribal and credit associations were chartered. The process fractionated some Indian groups, since the chartered organization did not have to be the officially recognized tribal unit. But the New Deal left the condition of the tribes of Oklahoma basically unchanged.

World War II changed life in Oklahoma's Indian country. The war transformed the Indian people and their lands in ways that are not yet fully understood. A whole generation of young men and women had the chance to earn coups in a distinctly honorable and decidedly Indian way. The old Indian songs were revived and new ones written. Indian warriors were sent off to battle with celebrations worthy of their heritage, while back home the new industries of Oklahoma needed workers with the skills and temperament Oklahoma Indians possessed.

Alice Marriott in her evocative picture of Kiowa life, *The Ten Grandmothers,* captures the excitement of what she calls "The War Party" (1942). Old Eagle Plume makes a ceremony for his grandson because "it's a long time since any of us saw the young men ride out and fight." Eagle Plume transfers "the power that my brother got in the Sun Dance and gave me." As the old man explains: "It is good power and strong power. . . . This is the power to go through war and sickness and all those bad things and come out safe." And then he sang the song his father sang when he was killed.

> I live, but I will not live forever,
> Mysterious moon, you only remain.
> Powerful sun, you alone remain,
> Wonderful earth, you remain forever.[14]

Afterward many who served in the national defense effort had the motivation and the chance to start new jobs and build new lives. After returning from the war, a Choctaw army sergeant beaded for himself and four of his Indian army buddies Indian dance aprons showing the state seals of their home states, Arizona, New Mexico, Montana, and South Dakota. His own was the beaded seal of Oklahoma with the state's symbols of Indian heritage placed on a field of blue. His niece explained his attitude. "The war," she remembered, "helped him understand that he could be a Choctaw, an American, and an Indian with friends among other tribes and other Indian people."[15]

Oklahoma Indians were generally unaffected by the postwar government Indian policy of "termination," whereby tribal-federal relationship was dissolved in an effort finally to "resolve the Indian problems." In 1959 the Choctaws, in what was thought by the tribe to be a move to self-government, secured legislation that the Bureau of Indian Affairs interpreted as "termination" of the Choctaws as a legal unit. In 1971 the Choctaw Act was repealed. In 1978, Oklahoma's terminated tribes, the Wyandots, Peorias, Ottawas, and Modocs were restored.

With the end of World War II began the process of reversing much of what had been done at statehood. It was apparent that what appeared to be the end of Indian tribalism was only a temporary lapse. In 1905, Hamlin Garland had written what he thought was a description of "the final council of the Creek Nation." After his visit to the session Garland met with Chief Pleasant Porter. "All we have to do now is put our house in order for the new tenant," Porter explained. "My nation is about to disappear." To the novelist the passing of the Creek Nation illustrated the inevitable laws of civilized society:

Nothing has been so revealing, so significant of the changes in progress, as this quaint and curious legislature, sitting in their decaying building, while to the ring of the trowel and the tap of the carpenter's hammer, white men are building a new, alien, and inexorable civilization around them.[16]

Porter, Garland, and the white men dismantling the Creek Nation could not foresee the turn of events that in 1976 would revive the House of Warriors and the House of Kings of the Creek Nation and re-establish the ancient Creek tribal towns as the federally recognized governing force operating under the Creek Constitution of 1867.[17] William B. Bryant, United States district judge for the District of Columbia, in *Allen Harjo v. Thomas S. Kleppe*, determined that the congressional efforts to abolish the Creek Nation had been ineffective and held that the Creek tribe had continued to hold sovereign status.[18] In 1976 the court found that the historical evidence showed that Congress had not terminated the sovereign status of the Creeks. Nor had it abolished the tribe's territorial jurisdiction; it had, in fact, preserved the authority of the Creek legislature and the basic government structure of the 1867 constitution.

The revival of the Creek Nation is a dramatic example of the widespread renewal of Oklahoma Indian tribal powers. Under the *Harjo v. Kleppe* decision more than forty historic towns are now functioning governmental units. A hint of the return to full nationhood for the Five Civilized Tribes had come as early as 1970, when direct election of the principal chiefs replaced federal appointments of chiefs that had begun at statehood. In the fall of 1979 the Creeks formally replaced the 112 year old constitution with a new document which reopened membership rolls and substantially reshaped the tribe's government.

In the 1950s the United States Congress enacted provisions for those state governments that wished to exercise state jurisdiction over crimes in Indian country. Under Public Law 280 the state simply exercised an option to assume the tribal criminal jurisdiction to operate courts in the Indian country. Oklahoma state officials assumed that they were exempt from the provisions of federal Indian law.

In 1953, Governor Johnston Murray, a Chickasaw, refused to meet with Orme Lewis, the assistant secretary of the interior, to discuss Oklahoma's assumption of civil and criminal jurisdiction over what courts defined as "Indian Country" in Oklahoma. In a reply to a letter from the Department of the Interior the governor wrote: "When Oklahoma became a state, all tribal governments within its boundaries became merged in the state and the tribal codes under which the tribes were governed prior to statehood were abandoned and all Indian tribes, with respect to criminal and civil causes, came under state jurisdiction."[19] The final line of Murray's letter is one that fifteen years later the *Littlechief* case proved to be strikingly wrong: "Public Law No. 280 will not in any [way] affect the Indian citizens of this state."

In 1968 the federal provisions granting state governments the right to assume unilateral jurisdiction over Indian country were changed so that tribal consent was required for state assumption. No longer was it possible for Oklahoma acting alone to end Indian tribal court powers. As United States District Judge Fred Daugherty concluded, "The affected tribes had to consent to the state's assumption of jurisdiction over them." The Oklahoma Court of Criminal Appeals agreed that the state could not operate Indian courts. Nor could the state try Indians for crimes committed against Indians in the Indian country.

The most important Indian event since statehood is the rebirth of Indian tribal courts in Oklahoma. That came as a result of the 1978 case heard in the state courts as *Oklahoma v. Littlechief.*[20] In this homicide case Judge Daugherty found that the federal jurisdictional restrictions on Indian country of Oklahoma had not been abandoned at Oklahoma statehood. Attorney General Larry Derryberry acknowledged that "the State of Oklahoma possesses no jurisdiction to prosecute crimes and offenses defined by the Major Crimes Act, committed by Indian against Indian, upon trust allotment lands within the geographic boundaries of the State of Oklahoma defined as 'Indian Country.'"[21] There is now by mutual agreement of Oklahoma state and federal officials a jurisdictional and governmental unit known as Indian Country which operates in the arena of federal Indian law and not generally within the Oklahoma court structure.

Indian courts have returned to Oklahoma, to an area whose

previous Indian court system had been seen in the 1890s as a model of efficiency for the other states of the Union to follow. In 1979 the first new courts began where the older Indian courts had ended. Browning Pipestem, the first chief judge, became successor to the Oklahoma Indian judicial tradition. The 1889 report of Agent W. D. Meyers, of the Kiowa, Comanche, and Wichita agency noted, "There has been little lawlessness committed by the Indians on this reserve and the offenders have all, when discovered, been speedily punished." The agent's general conclusion about the operation of Indian courts: "I can think of no other way in which as much good can be accomplished for the Indians for the money it costs the government [than] to sustain this court."[22]

On May 17, 1978, authorization for Oklahoma Indian courts came from the Enforcement Division of the Bureau of Indian Affairs to the Anadarko Area Director of the BIA in an opinion of the solicitor's office. The solicitor's opinion concluded: "Tribes may establish criminal codes and courts to control criminal conduct by Indians on restricted or trust allotments located in the former Oklahoma Territory if their [tribal] constitutions authorize them to do so."[23]

The establishment of Oklahoma Indian courts has already begun. The Oklahoma Indian Affairs Commission has declared "a state of emergency" to exist until the tribes have taken the formal steps to inaugurate the Indian court system.[24] Indian judges are now deciding cases involving their fellow Indians. Formal recognition and operation of Indian Country governance has returned to Oklahoma.

This renewed Indian tribalism did not come easily. When J. B. Milam began the revitalization of the Cherokee tribe, few Indians dreamed that an Oklahoma Indian government would ever again be a real government run by Indian people with sovereign powers and resources. The era following World War II saw the death of most Indians who had known the old ways of nationhood on the plains and of tribal governance in the Indian capitals. Men like Fred Lookout (1860–1949), who had become the chief of the Osages in 1913, kept tribal spirits alive, as did women like Grandmother Supernaw. A new generation of Indian leaders, men and women whose experience with the old ways was more emotional than actual, was now coming into being.

Yet the vision of the old ways remains strong with Indian leaders. A Kiowa veteran tells of being wounded on the Korean battlefield, where he saw a vision of himself with Medicine Wind, his grandfather. Grandfather told him that he would return to the Kiowa bluffs of

Oklahoma. The soldier "gathered all his strength and resources and dodged enemy fire, bleeding profusely and dazed with pain, but he held that vision and those words with him until he made it back to the safety of his airborne unit—and later until he once again stood on the small bluff in western Oklahoma where the restless Oklahoma wind swept over him."[25]

In 1946 the Indian Claims Commission came into being, and Oklahoma tribes began litigating many of the wrongs they had suffered. Oklahoma tribes who won land judgments were shocked to find that they were awarded the nineteenth-century value of the land and no interest from the time of the taking to the date of judgment. The state of Oklahoma has been slow to recognize Indian land and water rights. The Choctaws, Cherokees, and Chickasaws were forced to take their claim to the Arkansas riverbed to the United States Supreme Court where their claim was sustained. Other Oklahoma tribes are seeking the return of land and water. Such litigation has been long, slow, and disheartening for Oklahoma's Indians, especially since many of the old people die before the protracted court cases end. One Indian remarked that the search for justice has come full circle, back to Andrew Jackson ignoring Chief Justice Marshall in *Worcester* v. *Georgia*.

Some Oklahoma tribes have won significant judgments. The Cherokees, Choctaws, and Chickasaws proved before the United States Supreme Court in 1970 that the tribes own the bed of the Arkansas River between Muskogee and Fort Smith, appraised in 1976 at a startling $177 million. The Seminole tribe in 1976 was awarded $16 million for Florida lands. In a combined claim Kiowa, Comanche, and Apache tribes won a $35 million judgment in 1975. The Seneca-Cayugas received a $42,000 judgment in 1975; the Sac and Fox, $1.9 million in 1974; the Senecas, $5.4 million in 1973; and the Poncas, $1 million in 1973. In 1972 the Osages were awarded $13.2 million; the Seminoles, $12.2 million; the Delawares, $1.4 million; the Poncas, $1.8 million; and the Cherokees, $16 million.[26]

The irony of these claims is that, while the dollar return to an individual is small, the funds stimulated a renewed sense of Indianness among many people who had never claimed to be Indian and among others who were no doubt "payment Indians" as well as lily-whites and former black slaves. Perhaps this is also at the heart of the erroneous but prevailing myth of the federal support checks sent to Indians each month. Such judgment funds have stimulated a number of significant tribal programs, including those that build heritage and pride like the Creek and Cherokee cultural centers.

Since the end of World War II, Oklahoma Indians have produced a number of national Indian leaders, particularly in the early days of the National Council of American Indians. Claims Commission lawyers such as Earl Boyd Pierce and Policy Review Commission member Jake Whitecrow are well known, outspoken, and upon occasion highly controversial. The Americans for Indian Opportunity is an organization under the direction of Oklahoma Comanche LaDonna Harris.

The most dramatic Oklahoma Indian figure in the new leadership was Clyde Warrior, a Ponca, who was president of the National Indian Youth Council. Alvin M. Josephy, Jr., wrote of Warrior that his "utterances and writings made him almost a legendary hero to young Indians throughout the country before his untimely death in 1968."[27] Warrior's most famous statement, "Which One Are You? Five Types of Young Indians," set the tone for the early stages of the Red Power movement. Among these types were the slob or hood, the joker, the redskin "white-noser" or sell-out, the ultra-pseudo-Indian, and the angry nationalist. None of these, he thought, was the ideal Indian. Warrior called for leadership from educated Indian college youth: "Not from those who are ashamed, or those who have sold out, or those who do not understand true Indianism. Only from those with pride and love and understanding of the People and the People's ways from which they came can this evolve."[28]

Oklahoma Indians have endured the postwar programs of relocation, urbanization, termination, federal housing and health administration, the War on Poverty, the Office of Economic Opportunity, and even court litigation on the length of Indians' hair in the public schools. And yet the Oklahoma Indian remains, from the statistical standpoint of the evaluations of white society, poor, underemployed, and suffering serious health problems, infant mortality, and alcoholism. The renewed power and influence of Indian tribes is now being directed toward these problems. In this era of the new federal program of "Indian self-determination" these economic and social issues will provide a real test for Oklahoma Indian leadership.

In an age of increased Indian militancy the Oklahoma Indians are a paradox. No Indian peoples have been as outspoken or as successful in the use of the white man's court and government system. A further and equally important factor in the Oklahoma brand of Indian militancy is the absence of the traditional reservation to which young Indians from urban areas return, often alienated from the outside world and hostile to an entrenched, often religiously dominated traditional power structure. The Bureau of Indian Affairs has not so often found itself arbitrating or establishing tribal governmental leadership in Oklahoma as it has elsewhere. Thus even the most aggressive young Oklahoma Indians have not been confronted in the manner of many reservation tribes. The strange blend of Quanah Parker and Chitto Harjo produces LaDonna Harrises and Clyde Warriors, who opt for the conference and courtroom more often than the street corner or the bunker. Oklahoma Indians— plains, woodland, prairie, warriors, and Civilized tribesmen—have much in common in their expectations of themselves and society at large. The tribes expect, as Justice Black said, "great nations like great men to keep their word."

Most discussions of modern Oklahoma Indians begin with a recitation of names of distinguished Oklahoma Indian figures of national reputation.[29] Something of Oklahoma's perception of itself as an Indian state is shown by the fact that the two state statues in the United States Hall of Fame are of Indians. Sequoyah as creator of the Cherokee syllabary is credited with bringing literacy to his people. Will Rogers is remembered for bringing laughter to all people. The great Sac and Fox athlete Jim Thorpe joins Sequoyah and Rogers among Charles Banks Wilson's portraits of great Oklahomans at the Oklahoma State Capitol.

The Kaw allotment of Charles Curtis, the Kansas senator and vice-president of the United States (1929–33), is in the old Cherokee Outlet in central Oklahoma. One of the most dramatic and significant Indians of the late nineteenth and early twentieth centuries is Quanah Parker, the Comanche whose star-painted house came to symbolize the new Indian. The poignant and tragic life of Geronimo ended in southwestern Oklahoma, where this great Apache leader now rests. The Indian Robert L. Owen was chosen the first United States senator from Oklahoma. Admiral J. J. ("Jocko") Clark became a great naval hero of World War II, as did Clarence W. Tinker, of the Osage Nation, killed in action as the commanding general of the air forces in Hawaii in 1942.

The artistry of great Oklahoma Indian ballerinas—Yvonne Chouteau, Maria Tallchief, Marjorie Tallchief, Rozella Hightower, and Moscelyne Larkin—is proclaimed throughout the world. Oklahoma Indian painters revolutionized a traditional art form. Louis Ballard, the Quapaw-Cherokee, is the premier American Indian composer.

Kiowa N. Scott Momaday is thus far the only Indian to win a Pulitzer Prize in literature—for his novel *House Made of Dawn* (1969). The musical *Oklahoma!* (1943), which revolutionized the American theatre, is based on *Green Grow the Lilacs,* written by Cherokee playwright Lynn Riggs.

In 1976, when the American Ethnological Society selected a group of sixteen native Americans for their study *American Indian Intellectuals,* two Oklahomans were on the list: Emmett Starr (1870–1930), the Cherokee historian; and John Joseph Mathews (1894–1979), the Osage writer.[30] The two men illustrate the problems of many Indian professionals, intellectuals, politicians, craftsmen, teachers, and artists born before statehood forced them to find an Indian niche in an increasingly non-Indian world. Starr was a medical doctor who had been elected to the last Cherokee legislature and had been active in the Sequoyah movement. He increasingly retreated from the new world and after publication of his *History of the Cherokee Indians* went to St. Louis to become a bookseller. He remained there until his death. Mathews was an aviator in World War I; went to Oxford, where he took a degree in 1923; and became for a time an aimless wanderer in Europe and Africa. On safari in North Africa one night Mathews forced himself to think about his life. In so doing, he set himself on the road to becoming the premier American Indian writer of the first half of the twentieth century (to be followed in that position by another Oklahoma Indian, the Kiowa N. Scott Momaday):

> That night I got to thinking about . . . what happened to me one day when I was a little boy, riding on the Osage prairies. Osage warriors with only their breechclouts and their guns had come up and surrounded us—firing. Of course, I knew some of them, about them; they knew me who I was. That's what we called joy shooting, you see, just joy. So, I got homesick, and I thought, what am I doing over here? Why don't I go back and take some interest in my people? Why not go back to the Osages? They've got culture. So, I came back.[31]

Muriel Wright, the Choctaw granddaughter of Chief Allen Wright, eloquently stated the popular view of the Oklahoma Indian as articulated by the first and second generations of assimilationist historians. "Nowhere else," she noted, "can be found such blending of the blood and the civilization of the Anglo-American and the American Indian." In 1951, Wright introduced her *Guide to the Indian Tribes of Oklahoma* with a summary of those attitudes, which echoed many of the popular and scholarly discussions of Oklahoma Indians. "Most Indians in Oklahoma are modern Americans in customs, habits, and dress," she observed. "Some of the outstanding leaders in business and professional life as well as officials of the state have been and are of Indian descent. . . . The unique experiment of the removal of the Indian tribes to Oklahoma . . . has resulted in a degree of mutual tolerance, understanding and affection between two races which has no counterpart elsewhere in America."[32]

Many later Indian and white anthropologists and historians espouse a view in contrast to that of Wright and other assimilationists. The resilience and survival of the distinctly Indian element of Indian culture is now recognized. Conflicts between Indian and white viewpoints are no longer dismissed. These ideas are not a new militancy but reflect the scholarship of such pioneering chroniclers as Angie Debo. To this scholar the facts suggest that "the magnitude of plunder and the rapidity of spoliation" of Oklahoma's Indian people by the white citizen is without parallel anywhere else in the country.[33] The traditional Oklahoma story of Indian-white cooperation should be evaluated in light of the accounts of "forgery, embezzlement, criminal conspiracy, and other crimes against Indian property continued with monotonous regularity." As Debo concludes, "such treatment of an independent people by a great imperial power would have aroused international condemnation . . . but the Indians had been forced to accept the perilous gift of American citizenship and they were despoiled individually under the forms of existing law."

On Memorial Day each spring some of Oklahoma's traditional Indian people gather in the Cherokee Mountains at Chewey to clean the graves of their ancestors and to play ball and dance. On those occasions a prayer is spoken under the great tree in the cemetery. It is a prayer of the past and a prayer of the future. The spring is brighter now. The old fire of tribal power is renewed and rekindled. The Indian past and the Oklahoma present are coming together in new courts and revived tribal programs. In 1903 the Creek Chief Pleasant Porter told the Board of Indian Commissioners that the Indian people were "dying off pretty fast." There was, he thought, no special cause, no new disease—nothing, he concluded, "other than the want of hope."[34] For the Oklahoma Indian renewed tribal power brings that spring of hope, a revived and renewed spirit of Indianness.

Regardless of blame or fault, Oklahoma and its Indians are very different kinds of people from those Washington Irving visited. Long after Oklahoma's statehood and toward the end of her life, Spear

Woman was driven by her granddaughter to the Washita game range to see the fenced buffalo that in her youth had roamed the prairie as freely as had her people, the Kiowas. As the old woman sat in the car, she saw the great beasts behind their fence, and "she who had never made a song before found words in her heart and sang them aloud":

> Once we were all free on the prairies together.
> Blue and rose and yellow prairies like this one.
> We ran and chased and hunted.
> You were good to us.
> You gave us food and clothes and houses.
> Now we are all old.
> We are tied.
> But our minds are not tied.
> We can remember the old days.
> We can say to each other,
> Those times were good.[35]

Whatever the future brings, there is no longer the question of survival, no longer the danger that the strong winds of Oklahoma's spring will blow away the sustaining vision of the bright autumn of Oklahoma's Indian nationhood.

FRISCO LINE

A FEW FACTS
CONCERNING THE NEXT
OPENING
OF
INDIAN LANDS

B. F. YOAKUM,
President and General Manager.

BRYAN SNYDER,
General Passenger Agent.

St. Louis, Mo.

WOODWARD & TIERNAN PRINTING COMPANY, ST. LOUIS, MO.

THE
Great Kiowa=Comanche
COUNTRY

FRISCO
SYSTEM

Railroad settlement-promotion literature. The opening of Indian lands provided an opportunity for railroads to earn profits from speculation, as well as transportation. The Apache leader Geronimo was taken as a prisoner to Fort Sill. Courtesy of the Shleppey Collection, University of Tulsa.

The differing attitudes of the Twin Territories as shown in the Oklahoma statehood ribbons. The ribbon of the old Indian Territory proudly proclaims, "We were and are I.T.," while the Oklahoma Territory ribbon proclaims, "Hooray—Hooray—." Courtesy of the McFarlin Library, University of Tulsa.

Quanah Parker, transitional Indian leader. The Comanche chief was photographed in a formal pose in his "Star House" beside a portrait of his mother, Cynthia Ann Parker. Courtesy of the Oklahoma Historical Society.

Essapunnua (John White Man) was at the same time a traditional Comanche leader, a member of the Anadarko Indian police, and a peyote ritualist. Courtesy of the Western History Collections, University of Oklahoma Library.

Seminole tribal voting, Wewoka, 1902. Individuals are lined up on opposite sides of the street to vote for principal chief. Courtesy of the Western History Collections, University of Oklahoma Library.

Indian politician. Many of the minor prestatehood Indian tribal powers like the Seminoles' Chilleyfish survived as tribal leaders after statehood. Courtesy of the Oklahoma Historical Society.

The *Peyote road.* Paul Mouse Road Goose is dressed in peyote regalia for this studio portrait. Courtesy of the Oklahoma Historical Society.

Members of a Quapaw family on their allotment. Members not only of the Five Civilized Tribes but of other tribes, such as the Quapaws, represented here by Peter Clabber and his family, acquired a prosperity envied by many white settlers. Courtesy of the Oklahoma Historical Society.

The corn road. Full-blood Seneca Star Young, a prosperous Indian farmer, and his wife in front of their house and buildings on their Indian Territory farm. Courtesy of the Oklahoma Historical Society.

Peyote Meeting, by Potawatomi artist Woody Crumbo. Note the fire, altar, fans, and rattles. Courtesy of the Philbrook Art Center.

The Jesus road. Osages including chiefs Bacon Rind and Fred Lookout honor Cardinal Hayes and Bishop Kelley at Pawhuska, Oklahoma, in May 1925. Courtesy of the *Sooner Catholic*.

Osage Catholics. A meeting of the women of the Indian Altar Society held in Fairfax, Oklahoma. Courtesy of the *Sooner Catholic.*

Kee-Too-Wah Cherokees with ancient wampum belts. The religious leaders of the Redbird Smith movement pose with Cherokee religious relics before a clan house and sacred fire. Courtesy of the McFarlin Library, University of Tulsa.

Line-Up and Numbers of Both Teams

Referee TOM THORP, Columbia   Umpire JOHN REARDON, New Hampshire
Head Linesman— FRANK "BUCK" O'NEILL, Swarthmore

THE NEW YORK FOOTBALL GIANTS
1931 (Seventh Season) 1931

Playing Number	Name	Weight	Former College	Playing Position
2	MURTAUGH	190	Georgetown	Center and Guard
3	GRANT	225	N. Y. University	Tackle
4	BROADSTONE	220	Nebraska	Tackle and Guard
5	SCHWAB	190	Okla. City University	End
6	FLAHERTY	190	Gonzaga (Spokane)	End
7	HEIN	205	Washington State	Center
8	WYCOFF	205	Georgia Tech	Back
9	SARK	215	Phillips University	Guard and Tackle
10	ARTMAN	235	Leland Stanford	Tackle
11	GIBSON	200	Grove City	Guard
12	CAGLE	170	West Point	Back
13	KITZMILLER	170	Oregon University	Back
14	SEDBROOK	170	Phillips University	Back
15	CAMPBELL	205	Emporia Teachers	End
17	BADGRO	190	University of Sou. Calif.	End
18	BURNETT	190	Emporia Teachers	Back
20	GUTOUSKY	190	Okla. City University	Back
22	MORAN	190	Carnegie Tech	Back
23	STEIN	200	Hard Knocks	End and Tackle
29	FLENNIKEN	200	Geneva	Back
36	OWEN, W.	205	Phillips University	Tackle
55	OWEN, STEVE	245	Phillips University	Coach, Guard and Tackle

HOMINY INDIANS
Professional Football Club

Name	Weight	Tribe	School	Position
CREED (Little Feather)	165	Cherokee	O. B. U.	Quarterback
ORE (Big Twig)	246	Navajo	O. U.	Tackle
CORN	175	Cherokee	Tulsa U.	Halfback
DAVIS	210	Creek	Haskell	End
SHADLOW	180	Otoe	Haskell	Guard
HAINTA	250	Kiowa	Haskell	Guard
SMITH (White Eagle)	241	Cheyenne	Haskell	Fullback
PIERCE (Running Hawk)	180	Seneca	N. East	Halfback
McGILBRA	240	Cherokee	Haskell	Tackle
BOUDNOT	175	Creek	Haskell	End
BIBLE	240	Creek	Haskell	Center
SPENCER	175	Pottawatomie	Gonzales	Quarterback
PEE WEE	185	Otoe	O. U.	End
McGILBERRY	180	Creek	Chilocco	Halfback
LUTTRELL	185	Osage	T. U.	Guard
BUCK HARDING	230	Cherokee	Haskell	Guard
CRAWFORD	210	Sioux	Haskell	Tackle
LEVI	200	Sac Fox	Haskell	Halfback
CHIEF FIXICO	210	Creek	Bacone	Fullback
BRAVE	190	Osage	Haskell	End

Hominy Indians professional football team. Note the large number of tribes represented on the team. Courtesy of *Oklahoma Today* and the Western History Collections, University of Oklahoma Library.

Caddo and Wichita Indian baseball team, June 1901. Note the varying racial characteristics of the team members. Courtesy of the Oklahoma Historical Society.

Motion-picture Indians. Members of Oklahoma Indian tribes often dressed in Hollywood costumes to appear in movies. Here a group of Cheyennes appear in a motion picture being filmed at Fort Sill. Courtesy of the Oklahoma Historical Society.

Stickball game. A group of Indians playing the ancient Indian game, not unlike the games described by George Catlin a century earlier. The men use the racquets and the women their hands to try to hit the top of the stickball pole. Courtesy of the Oklahoma Historical Society.

Chapter 4

THE SPIRIT OF A
MODERN INDIAN SUMMER

Summer is an Indian time. No Oklahoma Indian can ever look back upon life without remembering a long series of summers and summertime adventures. In his book *The Way to Rainy Mountain* (1969), N. Scott Momaday remembered the Kiowa summers at his grandmother's house with "a lot of coming and going, feasting and talk." Indians are to Momaday "a summer people who abide the cold and keep to themselves, but when the season turns and the land becomes warm and vital they cannot hold still; an old love of going returns upon them."[1] Among the Arapahos, Carl Sweezy remembered the movement on the plains when in the summer the villagers went "to higher ground where they could catch the cool winds" and see the vista of "streams and thickets and prairies [that] seemed to stretch to the end of the world."[2]

One Cherokee recalls summer because "we always ate the wild things." Indians, he notes, "sorta measured the seasons by the change in food," and so during the summer "my mother cooked on a big black woodstove we had out in the yard." When she moved outside, he remembers, "that was the sign that summer had come."[3] To one Oklahoma Cheyenne the summer was a time of the "great sunflower war," when young Indian boys found those giant alien Kansas weeds and turned them into great Plains Indian lances with which they dreamed of and played at the old days of driving the blue-coat soldiers from their lands. A Creek woman recounts her summers as long days under the arbor at Baptist Indian revivals, at sings, prayer meetings, dinners, and running-stream, cold-water baptisms.

The summer dance has always been a vital part of the Indian's culture, not just a pleasant diversion. Mary Little Bear Inkowsh's earliest summer recollections were from the days before statehood:

memories of the Cheyenne Sun Dance, with the hustle of preparation and the excitement of the ceremonies. She watched the young men with whistles in their mouths as "the knife pierced the skin of the young man's chest, making two holes on each side" and as the sponsor "thrust a pointed stick through each set of holes, tied a small rope on either end of each stick, and finally, with a longer, heavier pole, linked the loop on the stick to the center pole of the lodge." The drumming and the singing and the bleeding and the dancing were too much for little Mary, so she hid her face. Her mother made her sit up, saying, "You are a Cheyenne. This dance is called Standing Against the Enemy, and unless you can face an enemy you may be killed someday yourself. Watch how brave your men are." At the end of the ceremony Mary's present from the Sun Dance was a rawhide drumstick, which she kept because as a Little Bear Woman explained, "It is a great blessing."[4]

In its own way the summer of 1979 is for Oklahoma's native people as much an Indian summer as the Sun Dance summer of 1879. The summers are different but very much the same. They are times of family and of tribe. Scott Bradshaw, an Osage-Quapaw reared by a Kiowa stepfather, explained something of the continuity and the change in Indian life: "If my great-grandfather came to one of our powwows he wouldn't know what was going on."[5] Nonetheless, the spirit would be strikingly familiar to the Indian of old. The sense of family, the pride in heritage, the distrust of the pompous, the show of finery, the seriousness of the occasion, and the humor of the moment are the same as they have always been when Indians gather.

In early June in the summer of 1979 the Chickasaw family of Hughes and Cravatts gathers on Sunday afternoon at the home place, the family allotment along the Blue River a few miles outside the old Chickasaw Nation's capital at Tishomingo. Drawn together for a celebration, they honor the matriarchs of this large and scattered family. More than two hundred descendants have come home in large mobile vans and small imported cars. They range in age from almost ninety years to less than nine weeks, from dark full blood to light-blond mixed bloods.

Perhaps most striking to a visitor are the two large yellow John Deere cranes with which the dozens of picnic tables are being raised and then lowered into place. One understands from this display why the Chickasaws and their neighbors the Choctaws were the great aboriginal entrepreneurs, the traders of the Southeast. Fresh catfish caught from the Blue River is fried on portable butane burners in great black kettles, while a full-blood cousin cooks the traditional *pahsofa* of corn and pork on a wood fire in the ancient kettle which some say has been used for such gatherings for at least a hundred years. Sitting on the tables are rows of dishes of home-cooked foods.

A carload of Indian men go back to town because someone forgot the cornmeal. A group of young girls whispers secrets while a gang of little boys runs up and down the bank determined to find poison ivy. Almost everyone comes to the trailer to admire the new twins, the latest addition to the latest generation of this Chickasaw family. The women gather in little groups and prepare gifts to be exchanged and tell stories of indiscretions, some dating from statehood.

After the gift giving and the speechmaking, the crying and the laughing over shared memories, there is the saying of grace by three Indian ministers in two languages. Then there is the eating. Next there is the singing of hymns in Chickasaw, in Choctaw, and in English. And then the napping and more eating. And swimming in the river. And more gossip. And more tears. And finally, laughter and an agreement to return soon as a family to this Chickasaw home on the Blue River.

A sense of place and purpose, of permanence beyond mobile vans and foreign cars, permeates Indian celebrations such as this Chickasaw reunion at Blue River. In a statement delivered before the feast, Charles Blackwell, a great-grandson of the Chickasaw woman who founded this dynasty, expressed not only the Chickasaw sentiment but also the attitude of most other Oklahoma Indians:

It is fitting and natural that we return here to this place—this Blue River—to celebrate as a family. These river banks have known the happiness of new babies, the suffering of passing generations, the excitement of thriving enterprise and the laughter and love of a great family.

From this place we have learned to love; to love the sweet smell of the air after a summer thunderstorm; we have learned to love the evening time call of the whippoor-will; to love the early morning smell of a wood fire.

This family home has given us the strength of a husband and a father, the love and tenderness of a young Chickasaw mother, and the unity which comes between caring brothers and sisters and their descendants.

We are fortunate in these gifts. From this place we have been given a proud Indian heritage blended with the enthusiastic courage of the new pioneer. From allotted homeplaces such as this, our tribes, our state, and our Nation have grown strong.

Wherever the circumstances of time and necessity may take us, this place will always be ours. So, whether we return here in reality or only in our hearts and dreams, we will always gather strength from these tall cedars, these granite rocks, and this our Blue River.[6]

At the beginning of most summers a number of young Oklahoma Indians participate in graduations, a white man's ritual now also Indian. They graduate from high school and junior college, the state universities, and nursing, medical, and law schools. The presence of these newly graduated Indians is making a difference in Oklahoma Indian life. For example, the new Oklahoma Indian lawyers have begun to revolutionize the state's legal system. Almost a dozen Indians of almost as many tribes finished their legal education at the beginning of the summer of 1979 and joined a growing body of law-trained Indian people. Many graduated as a result of the American Indian law scholarship program operated over the years by Oklahoma Indians such as Charles Blackwell, a Choctaw-Chickasaw; Phil Lujan, a Kiowa-Taos; and Bettie Rushing, a Creek-Cherokee.

One student among the largest group of Indian law graduates in the history of the University of Tulsa was Ethel Krepps, a Kiowa-Miami woman who has written on the continued relevancy of Indian values in the midst of white institutions. In an article recounting the difficulties her grandparents had in adjusting to the white man's road, she concluded that, while "all the grandchildren are scattered now, . . . it seems the strong Medicine Wind which braced us against the changing world when we were young and growing has sustained us through our transition. We have kept alive in our hearts the influence of the strong but gentle ways of our people." With a natural sense of being an Oklahoma Indian, she wrote: "As we gaze at the college degrees and honors which we have acquired in the white man's world we realize . . . in our hearts we are Indian but our minds must of necessity compete in the white man's world."[7]

Earlier the two-year legal drama of Gene LeRoy Hart acquitted of the murder of three Girl Scouts ended in the state prison at McAlester when the Cherokee died of a heart attack. The funeral filled the high school gym at Locust Grove. Thirty cars of "Indian family" joined tribal leaders from the Kee-Too-Wah ancient religion at the graveside for the Cherokee service. "The old Indian way is still very much alive," Choctaw Garvin Isaacs, Hart's defense attorney, explained, "and the Hart case brought Indians together in a determination that these tribal ways would not be used against Indian people."[8]

Thousands of Oklahoma Indians living outside the state plan their vacations to come home for their tribal celebrations. Whether Comanche, Cheyenne, Kiowa, Shawnee, Ponca, Delaware, Quapaw, Creek, or Seminole, there is a time and a place for renewal, a need to call for strength from the arrows or the wampum. And there is also a time that brings together Indians from many tribes for powwows and gourd dances, rodeos and competitions, visits and quarrels, rekindled romances and revitalized disputes.

The summer and the summer dances bring scholars and tourists to see the Indians. But Oklahoma Indianness is hidden and confusing. Much of the Oklahoma Indian way is lost to the outsider because the Indian world is both public and private and upon the same occasion may be both. An Indian legend shared by many Oklahoma tribes says that certain Indians can become transparent, turn into leaves on trees, or become small enough to ride on a bird's wing. Oklahoma Indians have been remarkably successful in doing just that. Indians have succeeded in hiding many aspects of their culture or camouflaging things Indian so that the Indianness is kept from the eye of the tourist or even the scholar. The outsider looking for a buffalo misses the deer, the raven, or the bright summer sun itself, which are all very Indian.

Much of the Indianness of Oklahoma is hidden because the Oklahoma Indian does not conform to the white dictate of what is and is not Indian. A Boy Scout hobbyist in feathers and headdress is by definition Indian to the students of the frontier myths. But a full-blood worshiper in blue jeans, a white shirt, and Stetson hat holding up the corporate seal of the Kee-Too-Wahs is not Indian in the eyes of the western moviegoer.

Furthermore, Oklahoma has few of the great geographic mountain and desert movie-set vistas that proclaim Indianness. There is no Oklahoma Monument Valley. No Oklahoma tribes have been like the Pueblos and drawn a whole school of painters and poets to record and romanticize their cultural ceremonies, crafts, and majestic landscapes. No Fred Harveys have merchandized Oklahoma's Indian arts and crafts around a natural attraction such as the Grand Canyon. For all this most Oklahoma Indians are grateful.

Whites dream of warbonnets and buffalo when they imagine the Indian, but many of Oklahoma's Indian people have woodland or prairie heritages. They are the descendants of the front-line Indian soldiers of the seventeenth, eighteenth, and early nineteenth centuries. Their brave leaders were the Tecumsehs, the Osceolas, and the Little Turtles, the great warriors of the Senecas, the Shawnees, the Miamis, the Creeks, the Delawares, and the Seminoles. These tribes fought the bloody pitched colonial and national battles of the eastern forests and the upland rivers. These tribes learned early the lessons of adaptation and acculturation that allowed them to adopt some white forms and yet retain Indian substance. That these tribes survived is a testimony to their ingenuity. For they saw, paradoxically, that change was their only hope of survival as an Indian people. Their lifeways, the summer rituals and reunions, are no less Indian because they dance to celebrate the fire or the green corn and not the buffalo.

"To the Osage," Agent Miles observed in 1889, "the summer was the most important spiritual season." Miles reported to Washington that "the full bloods nearly all cling to a creed of their own, and a large portion of the summer months is taken up by many of them in the observance of their form of worship. They are very devout and earnest and will make any sacrifice demanded of them to obtain preferment in their 'church.'"[9] Ninety years later the Osages continue to gather for the summer. At Hominy, at Fairfax, and at Grey Horse they celebrate in the grand traditions of a people who "make any sacrifice demanded." One senses that the spirit of the Lookouts and the Bacon Rinds and the Pawhuskas is still very much alive. There is irony in the realization that many of the women feeding Indian friends and neighbors will soon be off to a Catholic church to work as hard for the altar guild.

On July 19, Cherokees return to the hills around Marble City and Vian. They go back to the altar of their sacred fire and the playing fields of the tall stickball pole topped with a wooden fish. The occasion is the birthday of Redbird Smith, the great religious figure who revitalized the traditional Cherokees known as the Kee-Too-Wahs. The celebration begins at dawn when the firekeeper offers prayer over the four giant logs of the fire, which have been placed in the cardinal directions. The services continue until the next dawn while all are at one with the great green forest, under the shadows of the trees, in the reflections of the fire.

The Kee-Too-Wahs gather around the great fire to hear their leaders tell the story of the Cherokees, of the ancient way, and of the path they must follow. In the afternoon the wampum belts are brought out and interpreted in Cherokee and then in English. Seated under the seven clan houses, the Cherokees listen as Chief William Smith delivers the Cherokee messages from the seven historic wampums. There are great games of ball and at night long, wonderful dances with sounds of turtleshells and calls in Cherokee.

The occasion is deeply religious, as Croslin Smith explains in the English translation at the afternoon service:

Rennard Strickland

On this day we come before the ancient eternal flame to honor the ancient way. Kee-Too-Wah will be here forever. We must teach the children. This day is dedicated to mankind no matter what he has done. It is our job to forgive. Yesterday is yesterday. Never turn back on God or this law or you will be lost. History is important but more important is to look ahead and to go.[10]

Also in July of each year Yuchis and other Muskhogean peoples as well as many woodland tribes, such as the Senecas and the Cayugas celebrate the Green Corn. At Kellyville the dance is preceded by ball games and ribbon dances and followed by a soup dance. A series of dances and ceremonies, cleansing and scratching takes place. At the center of this is renewal from the fire and the corn, especially the feasting on fresh corn, which is a taboo food until after the Green Corn Ceremony. This ritual life provides the modern Yuchis with identity: "The complex blending of symbols in the ritual blurs and thus mediates the contrast between the major opposites of life." Students of Indian culture believe that the continuity of such traditions is at the base of the Indian psychological comfort. "Without their ceremonial," W. L. Ballard comments, "there would be no Yuchis; the sun would no longer continue its journey."[11]

There is humor in all these activities. Oklahoma Indians have historically loved to perform, to play and dance for themselves or crowds, to "play Indian" or just play. Colonial Indians traveling to Europe, Geronimo at the St. Louis World's Fair, the professional Indian dance troupe, the Osage ballerinas, Indians in Pawnee Bill's and the 101 Ranch shows are all part of the same tradition. The great Indian professional football teams, Oklahoma's long list of Indian athletes, the successful Plains Indian baseball teams, and the most famous of all twentieth-century sports figures, Jim Thorpe, are reflected in modern Indian teams and professional athletes. No competitive sport in the world can be as exciting as a Sunday afternoon stickball game back in the Oklahoma hills. Nor can any group of actors be as proud or arrogant as a group of Oklahoma Indians dressed by a Hollywood director in make-believe Indian costumes. If what one sees of the dances and the dancers, of the Indians at play, is just the outward performance, then one misses the spirit of the real world of Oklahoma's Indian people.

One senses the deeper meaning of the summer and the summer's dance for the Oklahoma Indian in "The Grandfather People," a poem by Kate Smith written about her Delaware people but reflective of many of the state's other tribes:

The Walum Olum has been lost
or destroyed. . . .

Your record of greatness, proof
of statesmanship and culture are gone. . . .

Your loss in status from Indian who gave
to Indians hunted down like animals.

Your loss in land from twenty million acres
to a final few in "Indian Territory."

The waves echo,
The waves echo,

"Tammany, Blackbeaver,
Journeycake, Adams."

No longer proud, united people, but
broken treaties, forced migration. . . .

Disease and hunger
have defeated this proud people.

Today, many scattered and broken Tribes
are meeting, and are Indians when they meet.

And this alone is left, Reports
on Indian affairs, a feast. . . .

And then, the ancient
Indian songs, our dancing. . . .
Is this enough?[12]

Summer or winter, the daily life of earning bread and pursuing enterprise continues for the Oklahoma Indian. Summer does not dismiss one from office or plant or field, nor does it lessen the burdens of Indian tribal business and government. Railroad tracks must be repaired; department stores must be managed. Firemen must be ready for duty; Indian alcoholics must be counseled; tribal housing must be built. And thousands of government forms that are a part of the Indian business itself must be completed. Fancy dancing and the powwow circuit involves only a small portion of Oklahoma's Indians; the business of being a member of an Indian family and a tribe encompasses far greater numbers of Oklahoma's Indian people. In much of the even larger business of living, the Indian and the non-Indian face similar problems.

As the summer draws to an end, there is a last-minute rush of Indian activity, perhaps as a final effort to enjoy the summer or to postpone the coming winter. The end of August and Labor Day weekend signal the beginning of the end of summer. Caravans of cars descend on the fields at White Eagle to camp for the Ponca Powwow. Families set up camp and costumes are repaired. Dancers assemble, and concessions open. Crowds of whites as eager as the Indian to prolong these days pack themselves onto bleachers in afternoon temperatures often above a hundred degrees, and fight the humidity and mosquitoes of the breezeless night air. When the drums begin to beat, the discomfort seems worth the effort.

White and Indian alike come alive as proud old men, beautiful young women, arrogant warrior-competitors, and little shield dancers parade forth. A late-summer Indian dance is an occasion that is entertainment and enrichment, a dream and a memory, the end of summer and the coming of autumn. The Grand Award Painting at the 1979 Philbrook American Indian Artists Exhibition, *One Sunday at Shawnee,* by Potawatomi artist Brenda Kennedy Grummer captures the spirit of the young and the old, the women and the men at a contemporary dance. The men at the drum are singing and drumming, while the women line up under the giant trees in sight of the American flag.[13]

Choctaws gather around the old national capitol at Tuskahoma for the Labor Day homecoming, or what is called the Choctaw Holiday. Today most tribes can easily get buffalo meat for their festivities, and so even Oklahoma Indian people who have not hunted buffalo for a century or more often roast or barbecue it. Outsiders unfamiliar with Oklahoma Indians may dismiss a meeting like this as non-Indian because there are no fancy feathered Plains dancers. There are stickball games and prayers in Choctaw and displays of arts and crafts and roasted buffalo. Visitors would be wrong not to see that there is much that is Indian here, more than just a darker skin and a few native-language speakers. The occasion is as much political as it is social, or perhaps among most Oklahoma Indians, and especially the Choctaws, they are the same. Politics, whether Seminole, Delaware, Shawnee, or Osage, form much of Oklahoma Indian life. And in many ways Indian politics is a deeper and more significantly Indian aspect of the Oklahoma heritage than the dances at Anadarko or the Miss Indian America contest.

To Oklahoma Indians the seasons still matter. To a people who are a part of the cycles of life of this planet, who live beyond and above the artificial atmosphere of central heating and cooling and outside the control of packaged food and preplanned public entertainment, the seasons are a measure of life. To the Oklahoma Indian the summer brings more than oppressive heat and fresh tomatoes; it brings to life a world of family, tribe, politics, tradition, and ceremony. In its way this world is as Indian, as real for this modern Oklahoma Indian, as the world of his ancestors ever could be. As one young Indian explained, "Being an Indian doesn't depend upon how you dress or whether you have an old Ford or a young pony. Indians in bright cars and neat suits are still of the eagle race and as the people of the eagle race we are still a proud people who have kept alive a great spirit."[14]

The crucible of Oklahoma, the sharing of similar historical experiences and government policies, has helped produce this spirit and the uniqueness of Oklahoma Indian culture. A great many factors have combined to evolve this modern Oklahoma Indianness. For example, most Oklahoma Indian tribes, as immigrant Indians, were separated from their historic homelands. Thus the strong and ancient geographic-cultural ties that nonliterate as well as literate peoples associate with landmarks are not present within the state. For a relatively long period of time before the Civil War many Oklahoma Indian tribes were free to adapt themselves and their culture to their new location without either the pressure of geographic-cultural ties or the presence of many external white pressures. There was a crucial period of time in which the Indian Territory served as a genuine barrier to the whites, with the vast majority of the whites who did live there present not as farmers or settlers but as appendages to the Indian civilization. The barrier was psychological as well as physical. There is also a history of tribal cooperation and intertribal meetings among the Indian groups in Oklahoma dating from the first half of the nineteenth century. Stimulated in part by decisions by the federal government to treat removed and reservation peoples alike and in part by a sense of common problems, these conferences reduced tribal hostility and stimulated united action.

The opening of Indian Territory to white settlement and the federal policy to end common ownership of Indian lands by allotting tribally held lands to individual Indians came at approximately the same time in Oklahoma history. They created a varied series of clashes and conflicts. The present-day absence of a large body of tribally owned land and the earlier federal failure to retain traditional reservations no doubt created a vastly different Oklahoma Indian community, as did the aggressive manner in which Indian farmlands and township lots were distributed by the Dawes Commission and subsequently sold with government approval. Therefore, towns with sizable white population pockets existed amidst Indian lands almost from the moment of settlement. The percentage of land in Indian hands was quickly reduced. Yet another crucial factor was the assumption shared by a number of Indian tribes, as well as by the state of Oklahoma, that statehood in 1907 changed forever the nature and purpose of tribal government. After statehood there was the national tendency to legislate for the Indians of Oklahoma, particularly the Five Civilized Tribes, as separate legislative units not to be treated as the Indian tribes of other states. Added to this was the presence of a great body of mixed blood Indian leaders that moved easily into the process of creating state governmental structures and in representing the interests of the entire state from positions of national or state leadership. Further, full blood tribal leaders chose not to move into Oklahoma state government, retreating and withdrawing from the state political arena.

Much of Oklahoma Indian life has been culturally bifurcated. Particularly since statehood, tribes have treated their recognized civil and traditional religious groups as separate tribal bodies. Thus uniquely Indian religious and cultural pockets can exist hidden within seemingly acculturated native populations. Other issues, divisive in many non-Oklahoma tribes, such as the role of women, have had little disruptive effect in Oklahoma, perhaps because those issues have few historic roots in this population. Oklahoma Indian women, many from groups matrilineal in nature, exert a major if not dominant influence in many tribes and certainly in most Indian families. Furthermore, Oklahoma Indian tribes have never developed a rigidly defined concept of "Indianness" and have therefore encouraged the development of divergent cultural strains. For example, there is little historical evidence of tribal division based upon degree of Indian blood. This stems in part from a strong degree of cultural confidence, a kind of native sureness that Oklahoma tribes define as Indian pride and some non-Oklahoma Indians regard as arrogance. The absence of factional conflict also results from a voluntary separation or cultural segregation that is geographically intensified by traditional Indian settlement patterns. Finally, the large size of the Indian population that is not physically identifiable as Indian but is of Indian descent in relation to the size of the white population of the state creates a kind of "Indian culturality" which exists in no other state and which, at least in the abstract, defines "being Indian" as socially desirable.

This particular set of cultural and historical circumstances occurred nowhere else in the Indian country of the West. None of these factors, taken in isolation, produced Oklahoma's unique Indian culture. Other factors, no doubt, contributed significantly to the development of Oklahoma Indian culture and values. Taken together as an overlay on the diverse tribal cultures of the immigrant Native American groups, these attitudes and events helped shape the people who are Oklahoma's Indians.

Today all Oklahoma tribes seem to be undergoing a revived interest in the old ways and an increased pride in Indianness. As Wayne Wallace, of the Indian Job Corps, explains: "Indians have pride in who they are and where they came from. . . . The values of Indian people are just as good and important as the values of non-Indians."[15] Yet numbers of modern Indians from all tribes choose to deny or ignore or forget all that appears to be native. Others retreat completely into the distant Indian hills. They go into an Indian world of the mind, hiding from the threats of the white world. Pam Chibitty Brazel, a Comanche-Shawnee-Delaware who works with Indian people at the Native American Coalition of Tulsa, notes that for many Indians adjustment is not easy. "Some withdraw into an all-Indian world shunning non-Indians and modern society, others 'sell out' and go on to the modern white man's world and forget their backgrounds."[16]

Within the life of the individual Indian are many distinctly personal values and attitudes which are nonetheless influenced by an Indian heritage. Between Indians of the same generation even within the same tribe there is no static view of Indianness. The world of the Oklahoma Indian is dynamic, varied, and diverse. And yet in some ways Indian culture is becoming increasingly pan-Indian in the sense that many tribes share such events as powwows, gourd dances, and urban planning seminars. It remains particularly family-oriented. The tribe remains an important element of the life of the Oklahoma Indian. The life of the Indian is more than dances at Anadarko, more than church-sponsored wild-onion dinners or public ceremonials. Events such as the birthday of Grandmother Anquoe or Mrs. Adair are at the heart of the real Indian world. Much of this personal Indian world remains hidden from non-Indian Oklahomans.

That the modern Indian lives in two worlds is a great cliché suggesting a kind of Native American cultural schizophrenia. The Oklahoma Indian, like the Oklahoma white live in a single world that balances elements of varying cultural traditions. The Indian brings another perspective to the resolution of problems. Into the one Indian life flow two or more cultural currents. The Indian thus plays many roles. Some of these roles are entirely consistent; others are hopelessly discordant. "Indian life does not fall into rigid categories," as one Oklahoma anthropologist noted. "It is, rather, a complex of interlocking circles, each exerting pressures and controls upon the others. An individual functions in different capacities in these circles or groups."[17]

The varied life of the real Oklahoma Indian exposes the bankruptcy of the stereotypic image of the Indian. The Indian lawyer in a three-piece suit can easily transform himself into a feathered championship fancy dancer. An elected county law-enforcement official returns to his office the morning after attending a peyote meeting. A nurse leaves the hospital and goes to have tobacco "treated." The computer worker has her house smoked with cedar. A man of 1/256 Indian blood sits in a French restaurant in Tulsa expounding the tribal genealogy, while the almost full-blood descendant of a great chieftain of the same tribe tells her high school history teacher not to tell her classmates that she is Indian. A gentle, hard-working full blood is pulled from his job and charged with harboring an Indian felon because as a religious leader he has followed the traditional Indian legal ways of his people. A nationally honored scholar-author consults his medicine doctor when a witch is haunting him. An internationally famous Indian artist tours China and Russia to renew her art. Such is the world of the Oklahoma Indian.

Patty Harjo, an Oklahoma Indian, asks the question "Who Am I?" in a provocative prose narrative. Her answer reveals the varied and mystical aspect of the Indian cultural struggle:

I was born of two heritages—both proud, both noble. They clung to their ancient cultures—one a wolf, one a snake—North and South. Their ancestral roots were transplanted to a new land of adjustment, grief, pain and sorrow, to a future unknown.

Theirs was a future that seemed only a candle in the darkness, a candle of hope for a new beginning. This was a land of disappointment. It was unlike the old. This was a land called Indian Territory and then Oklahoma. In this land, all tribes become one, all cultures and heritages began moving onward toward the sun.

Now our sun shines bright, our future is growing clear. We hide our grief, pain and fears. We are moving on. We try to grasp the good of our heritage. We try to grasp our culture that has slipped away.

We ask, "Who am I?" and our answer comes to us from the distance, "You are all the things you have ever known and will ever know."[18]

115

The spirit of a civilization tells more than artifacts or documents do about the meaning of people's lives. Understanding cultural spirit is difficult, especially the spirit of a culture into which one was not born. In attempting to capture the spirit of Christianity, an old Kiowa man went to a missionary service, made a contribution when the collection plate was passed, and settled down for the sermon. This Kiowa, Old Mokeen, who had already given what he thought to be generous, rose when the request for more funds came, squared his shoulders, and spoke to the missionary in broken English. "Whatza matter this Jesus—why he all time broke?"[19]

The corn road and the buffalo road, the Jesus road and the peyote road are different, but the spirit with which one follows the road, not the road itself, is the essential test of Indianness. This Indian spirit, an Indian way of looking, of being, makes a quarter-blood Chickasaw or an eighth-blood Comanche see life as an Indian. As Allan Houser, the Apache artist noted: "Young people know they're Indian and they hear stories. I think these young painters are using symbols and the stories but in a very abstract way. . . . They may not even know they're doing it. Now that's part of being Indian."[20]

"I believe that there is such a thing as Indian sensibility," T. C. Cannon, a Caddo-Kiowa, once explained. "This has to do with the idea of a collective history. It's reflected in your upbringing and the remarks that you hear every day from birth and the kind of behavior and emotion you see around you. It's probably true of any national or racial group that's sort of inbred."[21]

Blackbear Bosin, the great Kiowa artist, came close to capturing the spirit when he said that Indians "respect what has been created and they only want to sing about it . . . not duplicate it as if they were playing the role of gods." To Bosin the "whole tradition—language and figures of speech and even jokes—" teaches that "they can never be as great as the Spirit which created everything," and so "Indians do not want to take the real world into their hands and shape it."[22]

Why should Oklahomans try to understand this spirit of the Indian? What is to be learned from a remembrance drawn from the Indian? There is a pragmatic as well as a philosophical reason for seeking to find the spirit of the Indian. Our modern, changing world must understand the Indian's sense of place. The Indian spirit may help redefine the broader Oklahoma image. In the process Oklahomans may discover where, as a people, they want to go—at least understand the danger of aimlessly drifting. The stability of the

Indian may help Oklahomans define and redefine values in this world of change.

Among the ancient customs of many Oklahoma Indian tribes was a solitary, contemplative journey into the wilderness. An Indian went alone into the mountains, onto the prairie, or into the forest where he sought a vision—a mystical experience. While the quest differed from tribe to tribe, the object was the same. The outcome of the experience might be a chant for protection, a design for a shield, or a sacred and personal song. Yet the fasting and praying always gave the Indian time to think about a vision of life—an order of being.

The Oklahoma Indian can teach us to order our expectations of our relationship to each other and to our world. We do not have to go to the mountains to search for this vision. All we need to do is ask ourselves the hard, the difficult, the seemingly impossible ethical questions that must be answered to establish a rational order for our direction of society.

Without a value-oriented vision we are not unlike the sorcerer's apprentice—or like Mickey Mouse playing the sorcerer's apprentice in a feature-length Walt Disney cartoon. Too many modern-day Oklahomans have failed to search for a vision, a goal. Just as the nineteenth-century reformer's solution to the Indian problem was progress and advancement in civilization, modern Oklahomans seem to accept any movement forward as a progressive and civilizing achievement.

The poet John Crowe Ransom believed that progress defined as conquest of nature has no end. The result is a substitution of means for ends, a cycle in which one discovery, one new process, one new product, automatically, unquestioningly "progresses" to another.[23] When we do not exert an ethical judgment among the options offered by scientific knowledge, we are abdicating to the machine our human decision-making power, our value-ordering function.

Appropriately, R. J. Forbes, the Dutch technologist, closes his classic book *The Conquest of Nature* (1968) with an American Indian fable. During an eclipse of the sun the stones begin to grind, the mortars and pestles march against their masters, and all things mobilize. Forbes notes, "There is a tendency to catch sight of that same frightening vision" in our times and "to blame our tools for showing malice because our world has gone wrong in so many ways."[24]

Perhaps from the Indian spirit we can assert our responsibility to demand a rational order in man's relationships. The Indian has the

117

humility to admit that he cannot win an unlimited war on nature. The white man's concept of progress as salvation can no longer go unchallenged. We must have a vision of order. Ultimate goals must be ultimate in a rational sense.

The Indian sees a peculiarly strong unity between man and his world. The Indians have a myth, which the Kilpatricks took as the title for a wonderful book, *Friends of Thunder* (1964), which says much about the relationship of the Indian and nature. The relationship is, at best, a precarious one; but the friendship, the oneness, the partnership are there.[25] Loren Eiseley has written a beautiful explanation of man's relationship to nature that he calls "The Hidden Teacher." In that essay he describes a "long war of life against its inhospitable environment"—a war in which "nature does not simply represent reality . . . but [in which] nature teaches about reality." Eiseley relates the Plains Indian legend of an early people who were poor and naked and did not know how to live. Old Man, their maker said, "go to sleep and get power [and] whatever animals appear in your dream, pray and listen." That was how, in the Indian thinking, the first people got through the world—by the power of their dreams and the animal helpers.[26]

The Indian has a different way of looking at the world from the way of those who worship material progress. As the Spanish philosopher José Ortega y Gasset noted: "Two men may look from different viewpoints at the same landscape. Yet they do not see the same thing. Their different situations make the landscape assume two distinct types of organic structure in their eyes."[27]

Consider the forest landscape that eastern Oklahoma Indians confront. To many people the tree is only so many board feet of lumber; they see graded timber, stacked, ready for sale. The Indian sees in a cedar tree a mythical relationship of man and nature. There were in Cherokee mythology eight evil brothers. They "crept into the sacred circle of the Great Spirit who created the Indian people. Unable to know the wisdom of the spirit world, they stole from the circle magical powers contained in the holy relics." The priests followed the brothers, who ran into the sky and formed one of the constellations. One of the brothers could not run fast enough and lost his balance. When he fell to the earth, he became the cedar tree. Today the cedar oozes sap, bleeding for his evil efforts to learn the secrets of the universe.[28]

Another Cherokee tree myth concerns the fir tree. When the world was young and spirits ruled the land, a little fir tree was growing in the yard of an old man. The man was cruel and chopped at the tree with an ax. Every time he passed the little tree, the man would kick it. The tree determined to punish the man for his cruelty. When the tree got large enough to cast his shadow over the man, he would have his revenge. The years passed slowly, and the tree grew until he was a large fir. And when he was large enough to cast a shadow over the man, the tree summoned all his strength and pulled at his roots and shook his limbs. His trunk gave way, and the fir tree fell on the cruel old man. Even to this day the spirit of the fir tree of death rules the land. No one will plant a fir because he knows that when the fir's shadow is long enough to cover his grave the man who planted the tree will die.[29]

At the apex of contemporary Oklahoma Indian art is the wood sculpture of men like the Apache Allen Houser, the Cheyenne Dick West, and the Cherokee Willard Stone. When Willard Stone, for example, looks at a piece of wood, he has both the eye of the Indian and the eye of the artist. To him it is not timber, the first step on a new porch, but a story coming from the grain of an uncut piece of wood. One of Willard's pieces is *Young Rabbithawk*. In that wood sculpture the mystical relationship between Stone the Indian and the creatures of nature show through. The wood is smooth, and its natural formations make the bird's feathers, his face, and the heart on his chest. *Young Rabbithawk* also symbolizes the Cherokee Indian as he looks out on the modern world.

In *Culture and Commitment* (1970), Margaret Mead draws the picture of older societies in which the life of the youngest generation will be almost exactly like the life of the oldest generation. She describes a society like the traditional precontact Indian society in which there is little change.[30] In such a society the grandfather figure is most important. We, on the other hand, live in a society in which change is so rapid that none of the oldest generation has lived a life closely resembling that of the youngest generation. In such a society the value of the grandfather adviser is minimized.

In Indian society the grandfather was the teacher. Solomon McCombs, the Creek artist, has created magnificent paintings of the Indian grandfather, the storyteller, the teacher. Such a teacher would not be outdated in our changing society. The contrasting and conflicting roles of continuity and change in Indian and white society are highlighted by Erik Erikson in *Childhood and Society* (1950).[31] White American society "subjects its inhabitants to more extreme contrasts and abrupt changes during a lifetime or a generation than is normally the case with great nations." In settled Indian societies it is the grandparent—the grandfather figure—who supplies ideals and a sense of the continued validity of the family and the traditions of the culture. Using the Indian as the teacher would help American society through the uncertainty of modern change. We can look to the Indian as a grandfather figure for us all.

"Grandfather," a poem by the Oklahoma Cheyenne Lance Henson, conveys a sense of the continuing search for the meaning of heritage:

> the visions you never saw
> still deliver me from the void
>
> you stay now
> beyond
> where the snow is
> no longer pain
>
> wait for me   wait for me
>
> i will follow[32]

We need not become mesmerized into a new age of the noble savage, but we cannot afford to turn our back on the Indian's teaching. We need a quest for a new vision of life, a proper ordering of our expectations of science, a partnership with nature. The survival of mankind may well depend upon these decisions.

How can we learn what the Indian has to offer? We can begin by appreciating the philosophy, religion, art, literature, music, and dance of the Native American. Why are the tales of the Brothers Grimm, Hans Christian Andersen, and the politically minded Mother Goose a better fare for American children than the friendship of thunder and the origin of corn? The basic question is, When will we recognize Oklahoma's Indian religion, philosophy, literature, and the large body of native painting, poetry, and prose? The story of the Indian is the literature of America. It is not trite to say that the Indian sings the songs of our forests, of our birds, of our souls. His world is our world. He is of America. And he is America.

D. H. Lawrence, who came to love the American Southwest and its native people, said that the Indian will again rule America —or rather, his ghost will. This has special relevance in view of something that Thoreau said: The Indian has property in the moon. By walking on the moon, we learned that our salvation must come from the earth. William Brandon, editor of the *American Heritage Book of Indians,* has prophesied, "The business of the Indian . . . may turn out to be the illumination of the dark side of the soul, maybe even our soul."[33]

Joan Hill's painting *Child of the Elements* shows an Indian madonna and her newborn child cast against the sky and the moon and the stars in such a way that they are seen as one, a unity at once at peace with time and place. Joan Hill's Indian woman contrasts vividly with D. H. Lawrence's picture of the driven, frenetic American, alienated from his world and searching for cultural and political roots. Lawrence believed that the peace America was seeking could be found only from America itself. "America," Lawrence wrote, "is full of grinning, unappeased aboriginal demons, ghosts. . . . Yet one day the demons of America must be placated, the ghosts must be appeased, the Spirit of Place atoned for."[34]

Oklahoma Indians are now watching white Oklahomans. All Americans, Indians included, face the crisis of urban clutter, pollution, oil, energy, and the environment. Events may revolutionize the non-Indian society of the "car road" more dramatically than old Indian society was transformed from the "buffalo road." As their fellow citizens contemplate a change of life-style, the Indian cannot help but feel a touch of irony. The buffalo road and the life the buffalo symbolized to the Plains Indian, the free-roaming deer, and the vast cattle herds that sustained the world of the Five Civilized Tribes were all destroyed by the white man's progress and civilization. Now the white man has turned upon himself, unable to curb his wants so that he may have created a society that will in the end destroy him. This crisis is, in truth, more than an energy or environmental one. The white man's civilization faces a crisis of the spirit, a great conflict in basic human values. The Indian experience demonstrates the impotence of government to reform life-styles and the tragedy of relying upon bureaucracies to supply oats and ponies.

Survival is a word that describes the spirit of Indian people as diverse as the Kiowas of the Sun Dance and the Cherokee of the Kee-Too-Wah fire. The Oklahoma Indian has learned the lesson of building and rebuilding a civilization, of adapting, of changing, and yet of remaining true to certain basic values regardless of the nature of that change. At the heart of those values is an understanding and appreciation of the timeless—of family, of tribe, of friends, of place, and of season. It is a lesson that white civilization has yet to learn.

Bridge between two cultures, ca. 1928. Potawatomi Anglin Moore, ninety-four years old when this photograph was taken, was born in the free-roaming days before the Civil War and lived into the age of the automobile. Courtesy of the Oklahoma Historical Society.

Oil and the Indian. Courtesy of the McFarlin Library, University of Tulsa.

McIntosh County Indian tenant farmers. The impoverished condition of many Indians who had lost their allotted lands was captured by Russell Lee, the great photographer for the Farm Security Administration, in his Depression era series on eastern Oklahoma. Courtesy of the Library of Congress and the McFarlin Library, University of Tulsa.

Indian boy between his ancestors, 1939. This young Cherokee boy, the son of tenant farmers, stands on an iron bed posed between elaborately framed portraits of his Cherokee forebears in happier days. The photograph was taken by Russell Lee outside Sallisaw. Courtesy of the Library of Congress and the McFarlin Library, University of Tulsa.

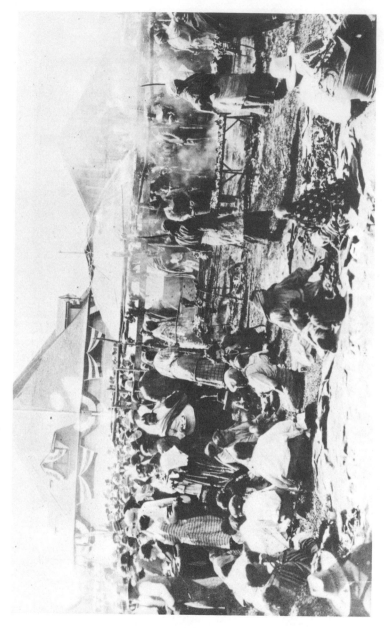

An Osage feast. At the height of the Osages' oil wealth the traditional hospitality of the tribe was not forgotten, and gatherings like this barbecue were common. Courtesy of the Oklahoma Historical Society.

Indians with refreshment. These two Comanches, posed in a studio photograph, are holding bottles of beer, perhaps an indication that alcohol is not a new problem for Oklahoma Indians. Courtesy of the Western History Collections, University of Oklahoma Library.

Carl Sweezy, Arapaho Indian artist, with painting. Sweezy, born in the age of the tipi, was instructed in painting style by James Mooney, the Smithsonian ethnologist. Courtesy of the Western History Collections, University of Oklahoma Library.

Indians in downtown Oklahoma City, gathered for a public celebration, ca. 1934. The tipi raised for display is outlined against the white man's skyscrapers. Courtesy of the Oklahoma Historical Society.

Feeding the ancient fire with the blood of the white rooster, 1934. A group of Cherokees gather to worship at the sacred fire. Photograph by Grant Foreman. Courtesy of the Thomas Gilcrease Institute of American History and Art.

Freedom's warriors. World War II revitalized Indian life and spirit. The returning veterans' renewed respect for tribal ways also guaranteed survival of the Oklahoma Indian spirit. Lithograph by Charles Banks Wilson. Courtesy of the Shleppey Collection, University of Tulsa.

The Cherokee drama *The Trail of Tears*, a symbol of the renewed interest in tribal heritage, is performed during the summer at Tsa-La-Gi, the Cherokee cultural and historical center near Tahlequah. This photograph was taken ca. 1969–70. Courtesy of the McFarlin Library, University of Tulsa.

Fancy dancer. The Indian powwow circuit and the dances have become important parts of modern Indian culture. This dance contestant is in competition at Anadarko. Courtesy of the Oklahoma Historical Society.

The modern evolution of a traditional society. The Kiowa Gourd Clan with Pearl Elam in the center of the group at a celebration held in Anadarko. Courtesy of the Oklahoma Historical Society.

One Sunday at Shawnee, a grand-prize painting of a modern Indian dance by Brenda K. Grummer, Philbrook Art Center, Indian Annual Art Show, 1979. Courtesy of the Philbrook Art Center.

The revitalized Creek Nation. A group of Indians attending a meeting to reestablish Creek tribal town governments, January 1977. Courtesy of the McFarlin Library, University of Tulsa.

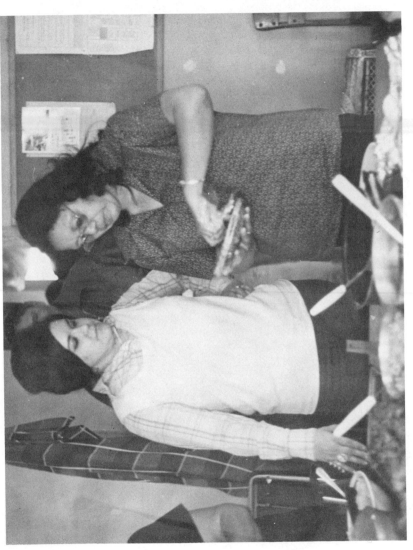

Preparing an Indian feast. Mary Schooley, of the Creek tribal town Concharty, and Frances Lowe, of the Creek tribal town Nuyaka, prepare dinner for participants in a 1977 day-long tribal organizational meeting. Courtesy of the McFarlin Library, University of Tulsa.

Young Rabbithawk, Indian wood sculpture by the Cherokee artist Willard Stone. This is an example of a contemporary Indian work reflecting the Indian's sense of oneness with nature and of the mystery of the creation of life. Courtesy of a private collector.

A new generation of Oklahoma Indians. This tiny Sac and Fox boy is prepared to dance at a modern Oklahoma Indian powwow. Courtesy of the Oklahoma Historical Society.

Shadow of the past and light of the future. An Indian father takes obvious pride in his tribal heritage and seems to convey this sense of family and tradition to his son. Photo by Guy Logsdon. Courtesy of the McFarlin Library, University of Tulsa.

BIBLIOGRAPHICAL ESSAY

Even the most conscientious student of Indian culture is faced with too much to read. Listed below are a few of the sources that discuss the general history of Oklahoma Indians. Many excellent anthropological studies, monographs on important political and social issues, and specific tribal histories are excluded, but use of the bibliographies in the listed sources will lead the reader to this specialized material.

The primary published source for Oklahoma Indian tribal history, cultural background, present location, governmental organization, contemporary life, culture, and ceremonials is Muriel H. Wright's *A Guide to the Indian Tribes of Oklahoma* (Norman: University of Oklahoma Press, 1951). This work, by the granddaughter of Choctaw Chief Allen Wright, who named the state of Oklahoma, lists alphabetically and discusses all the tribes associated with the state. The book also contains lists of readings for each tribe and a general reading list.

Angie Debo's comprehensive *A History of the Indians of the United States* (Norman: University of Oklahoma Press, 1970) is an analytical work. While it is designed as a general Indian history, the primary focus is upon the experiences of the Indian tribes of Oklahoma. An earlier Debo book, *And Still the Waters Run* (Princeton, N. J.: Princeton University Press, 1940, reissued and updated in 1973), is a brilliant account of the illegal seizure of Oklahoma Indian lands.

The Smithsonian Institution is in the process of revising and enlarging Frederick Webb Hodge's classic two-volume *Handbook of American Indians North of Mexico,* Bureau of American Ethnology, Bulletin no. 30 (Washington, D.C.: Government Printing Office, 1910–11). Many of the new volumes will discuss Indian tribes within the state of Oklahoma. Nonetheless, the original Hodge volumes are of continued value as a brief survey of specific tribes.

The story of Oklahoma Indians cannot be understood in isolation. Wilcomb Washburn's *The Indian in America* (New York: Harper & Row, 1975) and William T. Hagan's *American Indians*, Rev. Ed. (Chicago: University of Chicago Press, 1979) are standard historical accounts. Paul Prucha's *The Indian in American History* (New York: Holt, Rinehart & Winston, 1971) is an excellent collection of essays. Prucha's *American Indian Policy in Crisis: Christian Reformers and the Indians* (Norman: University of Oklahoma Press, 1976) and *American Indian Policy in the Formative Years* (Cambridge, Mass.: Harvard University Press, 1962) provide an unequaled picture of the American Indian policy that shaped the lives of Oklahoma's Indians.

A recent account of the national perception of the Indian is Robert F. Berkhofer, Jr., *The White Man's Indian: Images of the American Indian from Columbus to the Present* (New York: Alfred A. Knopf, 1978). Two earlier essays that explore the white image of the Native American are Ray Harvey Pearce, *Savagism and Civilization: A Study of the Indian and the American Mind* (Baltimore: Johns Hopkins Press, 1965); and Leslie A. Fiedler, *The Return of the Vanishing American* (New York: Stein and Day, 1968). A number of reprinted articles and photographs from the latter half of the nineteenth century are found in William W. Savage, Jr. (ed.), *Indian Life:Transforming an American Myth* (Norman: University of Oklahoma Press, 1977).

Oklahoma Indian history must be read within the context of all of Oklahoma history. The most perceptive and interesting observations on the themes and meanings of this history are found in H. Wayne Morgan and Anne Hodges Morgan, *Oklahoma: A History* (New York: W. W. Norton, 1977). Angie Debo's provocative *Oklahoma: Footloose and Fancy Free* (Norman: University of Oklahoma Press, 1949) remains an insightful account of the people of the state. Grant Foreman integrated Indian history into his detailed narrative in *A History of Oklahoma* (Norman: University of Oklahoma Press, 1942). Younger readers are the target audience for Arrell M. Gibson, *The Oklahoma Story* (Norman: University of Oklahoma Press, 1978), which contains an excellent selection of historical photographs. Maps that are crucial to the study of Oklahoma settlement are provided in John W. Morris, Charles R. Goins, and Edwin C. McReynolds, *Historical Atlas of Oklahoma*, 2d ed. (Norman: University of Oklahoma Press, 1976).

Original treaties and statutes for Oklahoma Indian tribes appear in the five volumes of Charles J. Kappler (comp.), *Indian Affairs: Laws and Treaties* (Washington, D.C.: Government Printing Office, 1904–41). Wilcomb Washburn has gathered many significant Oklahoma Indian documents in his four-volume work, *The American Indian and the United States: A Documentary History* (New York: Random House, 1973). Helpful primary documents are found in Francis Paul Prucha (ed.), *Documents of United States Indian Policy* (Lincoln: University of Nebraska Press, 1975).

Photographs, prints, and paintings are a valuable source of information about Oklahoma Indian tribes. Published pictorial sources include Robert E. Cunningham (ed.), *Indian Territory: A Frontier Photographic Record by W. S. Prettyman* (Norman: University of Oklahoma Press, 1957); Russell E. Belous and Robert A. Weinstein, *Will Soule, Indian Photographer at Fort Sill, Oklahoma, 1869–74* (Los Angeles: Ward Ritchie Press, 1969); Wilbur S. Nye, *Plains Indian Raiders* (Norman: University of Oklahoma Press, 1968); Emma L. Fundaberk (ed.), *Southeastern Indians: Life Portraits* (Luverne, Ala.: Fundaberk Publisher, 1957); and Thomas L. McKenney and James Hall, *History of Indian Tribes of North America*, 3 vols. (Philadelphia: D. Rice, 1836–44). Edward S. Curtis's photographs of Oklahoma Indians are found in his *The North American Indian* (Seattle, Wash.: E. S. Curtis, 1907–30) in the portfolio supplementing vol. 19.

A sense of Oklahoma Indianness is conveyed in autobiographical literature. Nature and man's relationship to the environment emerges as the theme of John Joseph Mathews's beautiful *Talking to the Moon* (Chicago: University of Chicago Press, 1945). Adapting to changing culture is faced in Carl Sweezy's *The Arapaho Way: A Memoir of an Indian Boyhood*, ed. Althea Bass (New York: Clarkson N. Potter, 1966); Thomas Wildcat Alford's *Civilization* (Norman: University of Oklahoma Press, 1936); and Alice Marriott and Carol K. Rachlin, *Dance Around the Sun: The Life of Mary Little Bear Inkonish, Famed Cheyenne Craftswoman Who Bridged Two Cultures, Old and New, Indian and White* (New York: Thomas Y. Crowell Co., 1977). A sweep of five Indian generations is found in N. Scott Momaday, *The Names: A Memoir* (New York: Harper & Row, 1976). Biographical sketches of a significant number of Oklahoma Indians are found in Frederick Dockstader, *Great North American Indians* (New York: Van Nostrand, Rienbald Co., 1977). A recent publication dealing with Oklahoma Indian leaders is H. Glenn Jordan and Thomas M. Holm, eds., *Indian Leaders: Oklahoma's First Statesmen*

(Oklahoma City: Oklahoma Historical Society, 1979), vol. 10 in the Oklahoma series.

Sources for unpublished photographs include the Oklahoma Historical Society, Oklahoma City; the Western History Collections, Bizzell Memorial Library, University of Oklahoma, Norman; the Thomas Gilcrease Institute of American History and Art, Tulsa; and Special Collections Division, McFarlin Library, University of Tulsa. The premier collection of contemporary American Indian paintings is in the Philbrook Art Center, Tulsa. Other excellent collections and public exhibitions are found at the Gilcrease Museum; the Five Civilized Tribes Museum, Muskogee, Oklahoma; and the Southern Plains Indian Museum and Craft Center, Anadarko, Oklahoma.

The poignant story of the transplanted native peoples of western Oklahoma comes to life in the pictures and text of Karen Daniels Peterson's *Plains Indian Art From Fort Marion* (Norman: University of Oklahoma Press, 1971) and in Dorothy Dunn's *1877: Plains Indian Sketch Books of Zo-Tom and Howling Wolf* (Flagstaff, Ariz.: Northland Press, 1969). The catalogue of the tipi exhibition at the Renwick Gallery, *Murals in the Round* (Washington, D.C.: Smithsonian Press, 1978), with comments by John Ewers, is a breathtaking picture of what Oklahoma Plains Indian life was like. Additional pictorial insight is provided by Myles Libbart (ed.), *Contemporary Southern Plains Indian Painting* (Anadarko, Okla.: Oklahoma Indian Arts and Crafts Cooperative, 1972); and Bert Seabourn, *The Master Artists of the Five Civilized Tribes* (Oklahoma City: Private Printing, 1976). A superb catalog with a fine narrative and heavy emphasis upon Oklahoma Indian art and artists is Arthur Silberman, *100 Years of Native American Painting* (Oklahoma City: Oklahoma Museum of Art, 1978). Acee Blue Eagle's *Oklahoma Indian Painting-Poetry* (Tulsa: Acom, 1959) is worth the reader's time, as are the discussions of Oklahoma Indian art in Jamake Highwater, *Songs from the Earth: American Indian Painting* (Boston: New York Graphic Society, 1976); and Dorothy Dunn, *American Indian Painting* (Albuquerque: University of New Mexico Press, 1968).

Contemporary Oklahoma Indians are the subject of a variety of pamphlets, articles, and booklets. There is important data in the Oklahoma Indian Affairs Commission publication, Ray Robert Gann, Jr. (comp.), *A Summary of Statistics for the Indian in Oklahoma* (Oklahoma City: Oklahoma Indian Affairs Commission, 1975). Urban Indians are the focus of James L. Red Corn and Garrick A. Bailey, *The Forgotten Poor: The Indians of Oklahoma City* (Oklahoma City:

Native American Center, 1976); and Susan Witt, "The Indian," reprinted articles from *Tulsa Tribune,* December 18–23, 1978.

The Civilization of the American Indian Series of the University of Oklahoma Press contains major monographs on most Oklahoma Indian tribes. The slim volumes on Oklahoma tribes in the Indian Tribal Series published in conjunction with the Franklin Mint are generally excellent. *The Chronicles of Oklahoma* (1921–present), published by the Oklahoma Historical Society, has included hundreds of articles on Oklahoma Indian tribal history. Two series of the Bureau of American Ethnology of the Smithsonian Institution contain significant tribal materials. These are *Annual Reports,* 1–48 (Washington, D.C.: Government Printing Office, 1881–1933); and *Bulletin* (Washington, D.C.: Government Printing Office, 1887–present). Almost every Oklahoma tribe is the subject of at least one of these studies.

Anyone seriously interested in Oklahoma Indians must be familiar with Oklahoma's peculiarly complex Indian legal history. Felix Cohen's *Handbook of Federal Indian Law* (Washington, D.C.: Government Printing Office, 1942) is the Blackstone of the field. A revision of Cohen, mandated by the Civil Rights Act of 1968, title 7, is in preparation. See Rennard Strickland (ed.), *Cohen's Handbook of Federal Indian Law: Revised and Updated* (Charlottesville, Va.: Bobbs Merrill Co., in press). A good introduction to Indian law is found in David Getches, Daniel Rosenfelt, and Charles Wilkinson, *American Indian Law* (St. Paul: West Publishing Co., 1979). A helpful legal compilation is William J. Wiseman, Jr. (ed.), *The Indian in Oklahoma Law: 1907–1977* (Tulsa: Private Publication, 1977).

Primary unpublished source materials on the Oklahoma Indian are held in four major archives in the state. The largest body of official tribal records is found in the Indian Archives Division of the Oklahoma Historical Society, Oklahoma City. Two major Indian research centers are the Thomas Gilcrease Institute of American History and Art, Tulsa, and the Special Collections Division of McFarlin Library, University of Tulsa. The Western History Collections of the Bizzell Memorial Library, University of Oklahoma, Norman, are a fine source of both original manuscripts and printed books. Indian tape recordings, oral histories, transcriptions of myths, films, and records are available from libraries as well as private commercial sources. The standard research key is Charles Heywood, *A Bibliography of North American Folklore and Folksong* (New York: Greenberg, 1951); and the major discography is Dorothy Sarah

Lee, *Native American Music and Oral Data: A Catalogue of Sound Recordings, 1893–1976* (Bloomington: Indiana University Press, 1979).

The Oklahoma Indian Affairs Commission can provide up-to-date information on most Indian issues relating to the state. Write to Oklahoma Indian Affairs Commission, 4010 Lincoln Boulevard, Oklahoma City, Oklahoma, 73105. Oklahoma also has area offices of the Bureau of Indian Affairs at Muskogee and Anadarko and the regional office of the solicitor in the Department of the Interior is in Tulsa.

The Oklahoma Department of Tourism publishes occasional booklets for those wishing to visit Indian sites within the state, and the calendar of Oklahoma events published in *Oklahoma Today* includes Indian activities open to the public. Oklahoma tour routes are suggested in the revision of the WPA guide published as Kent Ruth (comp.), *Oklahoma: A Guide to the Sooner State* (Norman: University of Oklahoma Press, 1957); and additional historic sites are found in Ruth's *Windows on the Past* (Norman: University of Oklahoma Press, 1977). Many Indian markers and monuments are described in Muriel H. Wright, George H. Shirk, and Kenny Franks (comps.), *Mark of Heritage* (Norman: University of Oklahoma Press, 1975). Dates of some Oklahoma Indian festivals and the locations of Oklahoma museums and Indian displays are found in Arnold Marquis, *A Guide to America's Indians: Ceremonials, Reservations, and Museums* (Norman: University of Oklahoma Press, 1974). The prime source on the Indian origins of the names of Oklahoma towns is George Shirk, *Oklahoma Place Names*, rev. ed. (Norman: University of Oklahoma Press, 1974). For information on Oklahoma Indian prehistory, archaeological findings, and sites consult Robert E. Bell, *Oklahoma Archaeology: An Annotated Bibliography*, Rev. Ed. (Norman: Stovall Publications, University of Oklahoma Press, 1978).

For further sources on incidents and general movements of the Oklahoma Indian experience or specific Indian tribal history, readers should check the readings in Wright's *Guide* or Francis Paul Prucha, *A Bibliographic Guide to the History of Indian-White Relations in the United States* (Chicago: University of Chicago Press, 1977), with particular references to other bibliographic guides. See also George Peter Murdock, *Ethnographic Bibliography of North America* (New Haven, Conn.: Human Relation Area Files, 1960), which contains tribal references. Other Oklahoma-related Indian bibliographies are

Rennard Strickland

Lester Hargrett, *The Gilcrease-Hargrett Catalogue of Imprints* (Norman: University of Oklahoma Press, 1972); Carolyn Foreman, *Oklahoma Imprints* (Norman: University of Oklahoma Press, 1936); Lester Hargrett, *Oklahoma Imprints* (New York: R. R. Bowker Co., 1951), and Lester Hargrett, *A Bibliography of the Constitutions and Laws of the American Indian* (Cambridge, Mass.: Harvard University Press, 1947).

NOTES

PREFACE

1. A general effort to explore Native American history from this perspective is Jamake Highwater's *Many Smokes, Many Moons: A Chronology of American Indian History Through Indian Art* (Philadelphia: J. B. Lippincott, 1978). For examples of Indian pictographic history see James Mooney, *Calendar History of the Kiowa Indians*, Smithsonian Institution, Bureau of American Ethnology Report no. 17 (Washington, D.C.: Government Printing Office, 1898); and Eli Lilly, *Walum Olum or Red Score: The Migration Legend of Lenni Lenape or Delaware Indians* (Indianapolis: Indiana Historical Society, 1954).

2. Rennard Strickland, "Rescuing the Indian Image from the Two Gun Historian," unpublished address, Oklahoma Image Planning Conference, November 1977.

3. Quoted in Rennard Strickland and Jack Gregory, "Emmett Starr: Heroic Historian," in Margot Liberty (ed.), *American Indian Intellectuals* (St. Paul: West Publishing Co., 1978), 108.

4. Karen Daniels Peterson, *Plains Indian Art from Fort Marion* (Norman: University of Oklahoma Press, 1971), 90–91, color plate 9.

5. N. Scott Momaday, *The Gourd Dancer* (New York: Harper & Row, 1976), 35.

CHAPTER 1

1. Jamake Highwater, *Song from the Earth: American Indian Painting* (Boston: New York Graphic Society, 1976), 102–11, with color plates of these paintings at pp. 104 and 105.

2. Count Albert-Alexandre de Pourtalès, *On the Western Tour with Washington Irving: The Journal and Letters of Count de Pourtalès*, ed. George F. Spaulding (Norman: University of Oklahoma Press, 1968), 51.

3. The published narratives of these travelers include Henry Leavitt Ellsworth, *Washington Irving on the Prairie or a Narrative of a Tour of the Southwest in the Year 1832*, ed. Stanley T. Williams and Barbara Simpson (New York: American Book Co., 1937); Washington Irving, *A Tour on the Prairies* (Norman: University of Oklahoma Press, 1956); Washington Irving, *The Western Journals*, ed. John Francis McDermott (Norman: University of Oklahoma Press, 1944); Joseph Charles Latrobe, *The Rambler in North America*, 2 vols. (London: R. B. Seeley and W. Burnsides, 1835).

4. Pourtalès, *Western Tour,* 53.

5. Irving, *A Tour on the Prairies,* 146.

6. *Ibid.,* 10.

7. *Ibid.*

8. Pourtalès, *Western Tour,* 51, 53.

9. *Ibid.,* 62.

10. See Map 1 and Table 1. An encyclopedic discussion of each of the tribes and their origins is found in Muriel Wright, *A Guide to the Indian Tribes of Oklahoma* (Norman: University of Oklahoma Press, 1951).

11. Grant Foreman, *The Last Trek of the American Indian* (Chicago: University of Chicago Press, 1946), 13.

12. For Oklahoma Indian prehistory consult Robert E. Bell, *Oklahoma Archaeology: An Annotated Bibliography* (Norman: University of Oklahoma Press, 1978).

13. See generally Philip Phillips and James A. Brown, *Pre-Columbian Shell Engravings from the Craig Mound at Spiro, Oklahoma* (Cambridge, Mass.: Peabody Museum Press, Harvard University, 1978). Major artifacts from Spiro are found at the Thomas Gilcrease Institute, Tulsa, on loan from the University of Tulsa; the Stovall Museum, University of Oklahoma; and the Woolaroc Museum at Bartlesville. A museum has been opened at the site in Le Flore County.

14. See Grant Foreman, *Indian Removal: The Emigration of the Five Civilized Tribes of Indians* (Norman: University of Oklahoma Press, 1932).

15. Foreman, *Last Trek,* 14–15.

16. *Ibid.,* 13.

17. A poignant account is found in James Mooney, *Myths of the Cherokees: Nineteenth Annual Report of the Bureau of American Ethnology* (Washington, D.C.: Government Printing Office, 1897–98), 125–35.

18. James L. Redcorn and Garrick A. Bailey, *The Forgotten Poor: The Indians of Oklahoma City* (Oklahoma City: Native American Center, 1976), 6. See Table 3.

19. *Ibid.,* 34–36.

20. See tables. The most comprehensive data are found in Ray Robert Gann, Jr. (ed.), *A Summary of Statistics for the Indian in Oklahoma* (Oklahoma City: Oklahoma Indian Affairs Commission, 1975).

21. Table 1 and Map 1; Wright, *A Guide to the Indian Tribes of Oklahoma,* 3.

22. Table 2.

23. Table 3.

24. In 1970 the U.S. Census showed 24,509 Indians in Los Angeles. Tulsa had 15,519, and Oklahoma City had 13,033.

25. Garrick Bailey, "Indian Population in the Tulsa Area," mimeographed, University of Tulsa, 1978.

26. Albert L. Wahrhaftig, "The Tribal Cherokee Population of Oklahoma," *Current Anthropology* 9 (1968), 510–18.

27. See Rennard Strickland, *Fire and the Spirits: Cherokee Law From Clan to Court* (Norman: University of Oklahoma Press, 1975).

28. James Mooney, "Calendar History of the Kiowa Indians," Bureau of American Ethnology *Seventeenth Annual Report,* pt. 2 (Washington, D.C.: Government Printing Office, 1893), 371–72. For additional sources on Plains tribes see E. Adamson Hoebel, *The Plains Indians: A Critical Bibliography* (Bloomington: Indiana University Press, 1977).

29. Mooney, "Calendar History," 254–364. See also Alice Marriott, *The Ten Grandmothers* (Norman: University of Oklahoma Press, 1945), 292–305.

30. George Catlin, *Letters and Notes on the Manners, Customs, and Conditions of the North American Indians,* 2 vols.(Minneapolis: Ross & Haines Reprints, 1965), 1: 64, 70.

31. *Ibid.,* 66.

32. Irving, *A Tour on the Prairies,* 28.

33. John Francis McDermott (ed.), *Tixier's Travels on the Osage Prairies* (Norman: University of Oklahoma Press, 1940), 184.

34. Catlin, *North American Indians,* 2: 65.

35. Carl Sweezy, *The Arapaho Way: A Memoir of an Indian Boyhood,* ed. Althea Bass (New York: Clarkson N. Potter, 1966), 16.

36. Catlin, *North American Indians,* 2: 70.

37. *Ibid.,* 75. For the particularly unique role of the buffalo in American culture see David A. Dary, *The Buffalo Book* (Chicago: Swallow Press, 1974); and Tom McHugh, *The Time of the Buffalo* (New York: Alfred A. Knopf, 1972).

38. Irving, *A Tour on the Prairies,* 173, 177.

39. Pourtalès, *Western Tour,* 55–56.

40. The nature of this woodland life is analyzed in depth in Charles Hudson, *The Southeastern Indians* (Knoxville: University of Tennessee Press, 1976). The classic study is John R. Swanton, *The Indians of the Southeastern United States,* Bureau of American Ethnology Bulletin no. 137 (Washington, D.C.: Government Printing Office, 1942).

41. Irving, *A Tour on the Prairies,* 200.

42. *Ibid.,* 41.

43. Strickland, *Fire and the Spirits,* 7.

44. John Stuart, "A Sketch of the Choctaw and Cherokee Country," typescript, John W. Shleppey Collection, McFarlin Library, University of Tulsa, 24.

45. *Ibid.,* 72.

46. See Annie H. Abel, *The American Indian as Slaveholder and Secessionist* (Cleveland: Arthur H. Clark Co., 1915).

47. See Grant Foreman, *Sequoyah* (Norman: University of Oklahoma Press, 1938).

48. For descriptions of these documents see Lester Hargrett, *A Bibliography of the Constitutions and Laws of the American Indian* (Cambridge, Mass.: Harvard University Press, 1947).

49. A convenient description of Indian publications is Carolyn Thomas Foreman, *Oklahoma Imprints: 1835–1907* (Norman: University of Oklahoma Press, 1936).

50. H. Wayne Morgan and Anne Hodges Morgan, *Oklahoma* (New York: W. W. Norton & Co., 1977), 32.

51. This analysis is based upon accounts found in Grant Foreman (ed.), *A Traveler in Indian Territory: The Journal of Ethan Allen Hitchcock* (Cedar Rapids, Iowa: Torch Press, 1930).

52. *Ibid.,* 79–80.

53. *Ibid.,* 113–17, 125–38.

54. Catlin, *North American Indians,* 2: 123.

55. The best account of the life-style of the Cherokee aristocrat is Carolyn Thomas Foreman, *Park Hill* (Muskogee, Okla.: Star Printery, 1948).

56. See Kent Ruth, *Windows on the Past* (Norman: University of Oklahoma Press, 1978), 4, 20, 34, 46, 73. See also, Foreman, *Traveler,* 88.

57. See especially the differences reflected in Grant Foreman, *The Five Civilized Tribes* (Norman: University of Oklahoma Press, 1934).

58. Stuart, *Sketch*, 33, 101–102.
59. *Ibid.*, 100.
60. *Ibid.*, 82, 90, 96.
61. Foreman, *Traveler*, 187.
62. *Ibid.*, 245.
63. *Ibid.*, 174.
64. Irving, *A Tour on the Prairies*, 22.
65. Catlin, *North American Indians*, 2: 40.
66. *Ibid.*
67. Irving, *A Tour on the Prairies*, 22. The standard history of this tribe is John Joseph Mathews, *The Osages: Children of the Middle Waters* (Norman: University of Oklahoma Press, 1961).
68. Quoted in Grant Foreman, *Indians and Pioneers: The Story of the American Southwest Before 1830* (New Haven, Conn.: Yale University Press, 1930), 107–108.
69. See John Joseph Mathews, *Talking to the Moon* (Chicago: University of Chicago Press, 1945).
70. Foreman, *Indians and Pioneers*, 106–107.
71. Mathews, *Talking to the Moon*, 244.
72. Francis LaFlesche, in Margot Astrov (ed.), *The Winged Serpent: An Anthology of American Indian Prose and Poetry* (Greenwich, Conn.: Fawcett Publications, 1972), 97.
73. Grant Foreman, *A History of Oklahoma* (Norman: University of Oklahoma Press, 1942), 7.
74. Barry Holstun Lopez, *Of Wolves and Men* (New York: Charles Scribner's Sons, 1978), 78–134.
75. See Karl Llewellyn and E. A. Hoebel, *The Cheyenne Way: Conflict and Case Law in Primitive Jurisprudence* (Norman: University of Oklahoma Press, 1941).
76. Jack Kilpatrick and Anna Kilpatrick, *Run Toward the Nightland: Magic of the Oklahoma Cherokees* (Dallas: Southern Methodist University Press, 1968), 109. The Cherokee headache cure consists of a song, an invocation to the wolf, followed by blowing in imitation of the wolf. When a Cherokee ran long distances, he made the sound of the wolf and treated his feet with a wolf spell. See also James Mooney and Frances M. Olbrechts, *The Swimmer Manuscript: Cherokee Sacred Formulas and Medicinal Prescriptions*, Bureau of American Ethnology Bulletin no. 99 (Washington, D.C.: Government Printing Office, 1932), 188–89.
77. Lopez, *Of Wolves and Men*, 112.
78. Jack Gregory and Rennard Strickland, *Sam Houston with the Cherokees* (Austin: University of Texas Press, 1967), 60–69.
79. Foreman, *History of Oklahoma*, 48–53.
80. William B. Morrison, *Military Posts and Camps in Oklahoma* (Oklahoma City: Harlow Publishing Co., 1936).
81. Mooney, *Calendar History*, 254–364.
82. See Thurman Wilkins, *Cherokee Tragedy: The Story of the Ridge Family and the Decimation of a People* (New York: Macmillan Co., 1970); Gary Moulton, *John Ross: Cherokee Chief* (Athens: University of Georgia Press, 1978).
83. The standard account is Annie H. Abel, *The American Indian as a Participant in the Civil War* (Cleveland: Arthur H. Clark, 1919).
84. Lynn Riggs, *Russett Mantle and the Cherokee Night* (New York: Samuel French, 1936), 146–53.

CHAPTER 2

1. The classic account of reconstruction in the Indian Territory is Annie Abel, *The American Indian Under Reconstruction* (Cleveland: Arthur H. Clark, 1925). For the coming of the railroad see V. V. Masterson, *The Katy Railroad and the Last Frontier* (Norman: University of Oklahoma Press, 1952).

2. See Douglas C. Jones, *The Treaty of Medicine Lodge* (Norman: University of Oklahoma Press, 1966).

3. Stephen Vincent Benet, *Western Star* (New York: Farrar & Reinhart, 1943),3.

4. Reprinted in T. C. McLuhan (ed.), *Touch the Earth* (New York: Outerbridge and Dienstfrey, 1971), 147–48.

5. "Protest Against the Establishment by Congress of a Territorial Government," 1874, copy in Shleppey Collection, McFarlin Library, University of Tulsa.

6. McLuhan, *Touch the Earth*, 88.

7. The standard popular account of Plains warfare is Wilbur S. Nye, *Carbine and Lance: The Story of Old Fort Sill* (Norman: University of Oklahoma Press, 1969).

8. Ray Robert Gann, Jr. (ed.), *A Summary of Statistics for the Indian in Oklahoma* (Oklahoma City: Oklahoma Indian Affairs Commission, 1975), 3–4, 10.

9. For a brief development of this discussion see Rennard Strickland, "Indian Law and Policy: The Historian's Viewpoint," *Washington Law Review* 54 (1979), 475–78; and Rennard Strickland and William Strickland, "The Court and the Trail of Tears," *Yearbook of the Supreme Court Historical Society, 1979* (Washington, D.C.: Supreme Court Historical Society, 1979), 20–30.

10. See the conflicting roles illustrated in H. Craig Miner, *The Corporation and the Indian: Tribal Sovereignty and Industrial Civilization in Indian Territory, 1865–1907* (Columbia: University of Missouri Press, 1976).

11. An excellent study of an Indians' many roles is David Baird, *Peter Pitchlynn: Chief of the Choctaws* (Norman: University of Oklahoma Press, 1972).

12. Jack Gregory and Rennard Strickland (eds.), *Hell on the Border: He Hanged Eighty-eight Men* (Muskogee, Okla.: Indian Heritage Association, 1971), 199.

13. At the time of the 1970 census about 32 percent of the Indian families in Oklahoma had incomes below the poverty level as compared with only 11 percent for Oklahoma's general population. The unemployment rate for Indians is three times greater than that of the general population.

14. Francis Paul Prucha (ed.), *Americanizing the American Indians* (Cambridge, Mass.: Harvard University Press, 1973), 10; D. S. Otis, *The Dawes Act and the Allotment of Indian Lands* (Norman: University of Oklahoma Press, 1973); and Rennard Strickland, "Friends and Enemies of the American Indian: An Essay Review on Native American Law and Public Policy," *American Indian Law Review* 3 (1975), 313–31.

15. Lonnie E. Underhill and Daniel F. Littlefield, Jr. (eds.), *Hamlin Garland's Observations on the American Indian, 1895–1905* (Tucson: University of Arizona Press, 1976), 46–48.

16. Hiram Price Typescript, Shleppey Collection, McFarlin Library, University of Tulsa.

17. "Annual Report, Commissioner of Indian Affairs, 1889," typescript, Special Collections, McFarlin Library, University of Tulsa.

18. *Ibid.*

19. *Ibid.*

20. Carl Sweezy, *The Arapaho Way: A Memoir of an Indian Boyhood*, ed. Althea Bass (New York: Clarkson N. Potter, 1966), 10.

21. "Annual Report, 1889."

22. *Ibid.*

23. Sweezy, *The Arapaho Way* 8, 41.

24. *Ibid.*, 38.

25. Report of November 1, 1883, in *House Executive Document* no. 1, pt. 5, 1, 48 Cong., 1st sess., ser. 2190, xi–xii, cited in Prucha, *Americanizing the American Indian*, 295–99.

26. "Rules of Courts of Indian Offense, 1883," pamphlet reprint, n.p., n.d., in Shleppey Collection, McFarlin Library, University of Tulsa.

27. "Annual Report, 1889."

28. *Ibid.*

29. Karen Daniels Petersen, *Plains Indian Art from Fort Marion* (Norman: University of Oklahoma Press, 1971), 130.

30. Wayne Moquin (ed.), *Great Documents in American History* (New York: Praeger Publishers, 1973), 110.

31. *Ibid.*

32. "Annual Report, 1889."

33. *Ibid.*

34. N. Scott Momaday, *The Names: A Memoir* (New York: Harper & Row, 1976), 29.

35. "Annual Report, 1889."

36. Sweezy, *The Arapaho Way*, 47.

37. D. W. C. Duncan, "Conditions in the Indian Territory," in Moquin, *Great Documents in American History*, 286–89.

38. The subsequent discussion of the Five Civilized Tribes is based on Leo Bennett's extensive report in "Annual Report, 1889." Unless otherwise noted all quotations are from Bennett.

39. Judge Isaac Parker, quoted in Gregory and Strickland, *Hell on the Border*, 15–16, 196–99.

40. "Annual Report, 1889."

41. *Ibid.*

42. *Ibid.*

43. David R. Wrone and Russell S. Nelson, Jr. (eds.), *Who's the Savage?* (Greenwich, Conn.: Fawcett Publications, 1973), 443–51.

44. Joel B. Mayes, *Third Annual Message* (Tahlequah, Okla.: Cherokee Advocate, 1889).

45. Earl Boyd Pierce and Rennard Strickland, *The Cherokee People* (Phoenix, Ariz.: Indian Tribal Series, 1973), 62–68.

46. Joseph H. Cash and Gerald Wolff, *The Comanche People* (Phoenix, Ariz.: Indian Tribal Series, 1974), 69.

47. Keith Ham, "Chitto Harjo and The Snake Revolution," unpublished paper, May 1979, Shleppey Collection, McFarlin Library, University of Tulsa.

48. Alexander Posey, *The Poems of Alexander Posey* (Topeka, Kans.: Crane & Company, 1910), 88.

49. Angie Debo, *A History of the Indians of the United States* (Norman: University of Oklahoma Press, 1971), 36.

50. See Angie Debo, *And Still the Waters Run: The Betrayal of the Five Civilized Tribes* (Princeton, N. J.: Princeton University Press, 1940).

51. Muriel Wright, *A Guide to the Indian Tribes of Oklahoma* (Norman: University of Oklahoma Press, 1951), 221.

52. The statistics are gathered in Grant Foreman, *A History of Oklahoma* (Norman: University of Oklahoma Press, 1942), 307.

53. C. B. Clarke, "Drove Off Like Dogs," in John K. Mahon (ed.), *Indians of the Lower South: Past and Present* (Pensacola, Fla.: Gulf Coast History Conference, 1975), 118–24.

54. See Amos D. Maxwell, *The Sequoyah Convention* (Boston: Meador Publishing Co., 1953).

55. Rennard Strickland and James C. Thomas, "Most Sensibly Conservative and Safely Radical: Oklahoma's Constitutional Regulation of Economic Power, Land Ownership and Corporate Monopoly," *Tulsa Law Journal* 9 (1973), 167–238.

56. William H. Murray, "The Constitutional Convention," *Chronicles of Oklahoma* 9 (1931), 126.

57. Oklahoma Constitution, art. 2, sec. 32; art. 5, sec. 44; art. 14, sec. 1; art. 10, sec. 15; art. 22, sec. 1; art. 22, sec. 2.

58. Edward Everett Dale, *The Range Cattle Industry: Ranching on the Great Plains from 1865 to 1925* (Norman: University of Oklahoma Press, 1930), 146.

59. The process of theft of Indian lands is explored in depth in Debo, *And Still the Waters Run.*

60. Richard M. Ketchum, *Will Rogers: His Life and Times* (New York: Simon & Schuster, 1973), 51; "Will Rogers," typescript, Indian Quotations, Special Collections, McFarlin Library, University of Tulsa.

61. Alexander Posey Manuscripts, Shleppey Collection, McFarlin Library, University of Tulsa.

62. Edward Everett Dale, "Two Mississippi Valley Frontiers," *Chronicles of Oklahoma* 26 (Winter 1948–49), 382.

CHAPTER 3

1. Alice Marriott, *The Ten Grandmothers* (Norman: University of Oklahoma Press, 1945), 255.

2. Elsie Clews Parsons, *Kiowa Tales* (New York: American Folklore Society, 1929), x.

3. See Charles R. Larson, *American Indian Fiction* (Albuquerque: University of New Mexico Press, 1978), 55–65.

4. John Joseph Mathews, *Wah'Kon-Tah* (Norman: University of Oklahoma Press, 1932), 332.

5. For Ghost Dance and peyote discussions see Virginia Cole Trenholm, *The Arapahoes, Our People* (Norman: University of Oklahoma Press, 1970), 283–309, esp. 294. See also Donald J. Berthrong, *The Cheyenne and Arapaho Ordeal: Reservation and Agency Life in the Indian Territory* (Norman: University of Oklahoma Press, 1976), 296–340; Carl Sweezy, *The Arapaho Way: A Memoir of an Indian Boyhood,* ed. Althea Bass (New York: Clarkson Potter, 1966), 76.

6. Quoted in Jamake Highwater, *Song from the Earth: American Indian Painting* (Boston: New York Graphic Society, 1976), 170.

7. Thomas Wildcat Alford, *Civilization* (Norman: University of Oklahoma Press, 1936), 198–99.

8. An excellent discussion of the Osage oil boom based on a series of television scripts is Robert Gregory, *Oil in Oklahoma* (Muskogee, Okla.: Private Printing, 1976),

53–59. All quotations are from the Gregory scripts. See also John Joseph Mathews, *The Osages: Children of the Middle Waters* (Norman: University of Oklahoma Press, 1961), 771–84.

10. *Ibid.,* 57.

11. B. T. Quinten, "Oklahoma Tribes, the Great Depression, and the Indian Bureau," *Mid-America* 49 (January 1967), 29–43; Congressional documents reprinted in David R. Wrone and Russell S. Nelson, Jr. (eds.), *Who's the Savage?* (Greenwich, Conn.: Fawcett Publications, 1973), 514–20.

12. Angie Debo, *And Still the Waters Run: The Betrayal of the Five Civilized Tribes* (Princeton: Princeton University Press, 1940); Rennard Strickland, "Friends and Enemies of the American Indian: An Essay Review on Native American Law and Public Policy," *American Indian Law Review* 3 (1975), 313–31.

13. Debo, *And Still the Waters Run,* 313; Gertrude Bonnin, *Oklahoma's Poor Rich Indians: An Orgy of Graft and Exploitation of the Five Civilized Tribes—Legalized Robbery* (Philadelphia: Indian Rights Association, 1924).

14. Marriott, *The Ten Grandmothers,* 278–84.

15. Rennard Strickland, interview with Helen Konar, December 1977.

16. Lonnie E. Underhill and Daniel F. Littlefield, Jr. (eds.), *Hamlin Garland's Observations on the American Indian 1895–1905* (Tucson: University of Arizona Press, 1976).

17. A new constitution was adopted by a vote of 1,896 to 1,694.

18. *Harjo* v. *Kleppe,* 420 F. Supp 1110 (D.D.C. 1976).

19. Cited in "Memorandum, Office of Solicitor, U.S. Department of the Interior, May 12, 1978."

20. Case nos. CR-76-207D (1977) and 0-77-107 (1978); 573 P.2d 263 (Oklahoma Criminal Appeals, 1978).

21. Advisory opinion, letter from Larry Derryberry and Catherine Gatchell Naifeh, January 4, 1978, Oklahoma Attorney General's Office.

22. "Annual Report, 1889, Commissioner of Indian Affairs," typescript, Special Collections, McFarlin Library, University of Tulsa.

23. Thomas Fredericks, Memorandum, Office of Solicitor, Department of the Interior, May 12, 1978.

24. Resolution, Meeting of the Board of Directors, Oklahoma Indian Affairs Commission, June 13, 1978.

25. Ethel Krepps, "A Strong Medicine Wind," *True West* 26 (March–April 1979), 42.

26. Susan Witt, *Tulsa Tribune,* reprinted articles, December 18–23, 1978.

27. Alvin M. Josephy, Jr., *Red Power: The American Indian's Fight for Freedom* (New York: American Heritage Press, 1974), 83.

28. Shirley Hill Witt and Stan Steiner, *The Way: An Anthology of American Indian Literature* (New York: Vintage Books, 1972), 108–11. See also Warrior, cited in Wayne Moquin (ed.), *Great Documents in American History* (New York: Praeger Publishers, 1973), 110.

29. See, for example, the Oklahoma Indians in Frederick J. Dockstader, *Great North American Indians: Profiles in Life and Leadership* (New York: Van Nostrand, Reinhold Co., 1977).

30. Rennard Strickland and Jack Gregory, "Emmett Starr, Cherokee," and Garrick Bailey, "John Joseph Mathews, Osage," in Margot Liberty (ed.), *American Indian Intellectuals* (St. Paul, Minn.: West Publishing Co., 1978), 105–14, 205–14.

31. Quoted in Guy Logsdon, "John Joseph Mathews: A Conversation," *Nimrod* 16 (1972), 71.

32. Muriel Wright, *A Guide to the Indian Tribes of Oklahoma* (Norman: University of Oklahoma Press, 1951), 3–18.

33. Debo, *And Still the Waters Run*, viii.

34. Angie Debo, *History of the Indians of the United States* (Norman: University of Oklahoma Press, 1971), 8.

35. Marriott, *The Ten Grandmothers*, 289.

CHAPTER 4

1. N. Scott Momaday, *The Way to Rainy Mountain* (Albuquerque: University of New Mexico Press, 1969), 11.

2. Carl Sweezy, *The Arapaho Way: A Memoir of an Indian Boyhood*, ed. Althea Bass (New York: Clarkson N. Potter, 1966), 10–11.

3. Jack Gregory and Rennard Strickland, *Adventures of an Indian Boy* (Muskogee, Okla.: Indian Heritage Association, 1974), 23.

4. Alice Marriott and Carol Rachlin, *Dance Around the Sun* (New York: Thomas Y. Crowell, 1977), 9–22.

5. Quoted in Susan Witt, "The Indian," *Tulsa Tribune*, reprinted articles, December 18–23, 1978.

6. Rennard Strickland, "Field Notes, June 10, 1979," typescript, Special Collections, McFarlin Library, University of Tulsa.

7. Ethel Krepps, "A Strong Medicine Wind," *True West* 26 (March–April 1979), 42.

8. Interview, Garvin Isaacs, July 19, 1979, Hart Files, Special Collections, McFarlin Library, University of Tulsa.

9. "Annual Report, Commissioner of Indian Affairs, 1889," typescript, Special Collections, McFarlin Library, University of Tulsa.

10. Rennard Strickland, "Field Notes, July 19, 1978," Kee-Too-Wah File, McFarlin Library, University of Tulsa.

11. W. L. Ballard, *The Yuchi Green Corn Ceremonial* (Berkeley: University of California Press, 1978), 72.

12. *The American Indian Reader: Literature* (San Francisco: American Indian Educational Publishers, 1973), 47–48.

13. See ceremonial photos and paintings in Charles Banks Wilson, *Indians of Eastern Oklahoma Including Quapaw Agency* (Afton, Okla.: Buffalo Publishing Company, 1956); Carol Rachlin, "Powwow," *Oklahoma Today* 14 (Spring 1964), 18–22.

14. Gregory and Strickland, *Adventures*, 29.

15. Quoted in Susan Witt, *Tulsa Tribune*, reprinted articles, December 18–23, 1978.

16. *Ibid.*

17. Carol Rachlin, "Tight Shoe Night: Oklahoma Indians Today," in Stuart Levine and Nancy O. Lurie (ed.), *The American Indian Today* (De Land, Fla.: Everett/Edwards, 1968), 107. See also James Howard, "The Pan-Indian Culture of Oklahoma," *Scientific Monthly* 18, 5 (November 1955), 215–20.

18. Reprinted in *The American Indian Reader: Literature*, 113.

19. Ethel Krepps, "A Strong Medicine Wind," *True West* 26 (March–April 1979), 40. Many of the ideas in this chapter are developed more fully in Rennard Strickland, "The Idea of Environment and the Ideal of the Indian," in R. Merwin Deever et al., *American Indian Education* (Tempe: Arizona State University, 1974), 204–10.

20. Quoted in Jamake Highwater, *Songs from the Earth: American Indian Painting* (Boston: New York Graphic Society, 1976), 146–47.

21. *Ibid.,* 177.

22. *Ibid.,* 158–59.

23. John Crowe Ransom, "Reconstructed but Unregenerated," in *I'll Take My Stand* (New York: Harper & Row Torchbooks, 1962), 7–10.

24. R. J. Forbes, *The Conquest of Nature: Technology and Its Consequences* (New York: New American Library, 1968), 135–36.

25. Jack F. Kilpatrick and Anna G. Kilpatrick, *Friends of Thunder: Folktales of the Oklahoma Cherokees* (Dallas: Southern Methodist University Press, 1964).

26. Loren Eiseley, *The Unexpected Universe* (New York: Harcourt, Brace, and World, 1969), 56.

27. José Ortega y Gasset, *The Modern Theme* (New York: Harper & Row Torchbooks, 1961), 89.

28. John Howard Payne Manuscripts, Unpublished Journals, Ayer Collection, Newberry Library, Chicago.

29. Jack Gregory and Rennard Strickland, *Cherokee Spirit Tales* (Fayetteville, Ark.: Indian Heritage Association, 1969), 17.

30. See generally Margaret Mead, *Culture and Commitment: A Study of the Generation Gap* (Garden City, N. Y.: Natural History Press, Doubleday & Co., 1970), 1–31.

31. Erik H. Erikson, *Childhood and Society* (New York: W. W. Norton, 1950), 244, 271. For the particular application to Indian culture see chap. 3, "Hunters Across the Prairie," and chap. 4, "Fishermen Along a Salmon River."

32. Reprinted in Duane Niatum (ed.), *Carriers of the Dream Wheel: Contemporary Native American Poetry* (New York: Harper & Row, 1975), 62.

33. William Brandon, "American Indians: The Real American Revolution," *Progressive* 34 (February 1970), 30.

34. For much of Lawrence's work on the American Indian see Edward D. McDonald (ed.), *Phoenix: The Posthumous Papers of D. H. Lawrence* (New York: Viking Press, 1964), 87–103, 117–18, 141–50. D. H. Lawrence's insightful analysis of the demon of the American Indian in James Fenimore Cooper and in American society is found in his *Studies in Classic American Literature* (New York: T. Seltzer, 1923), 67–92.

TABLES

Table 1.   Indian Tribes of Oklahoma

Alabama	Illinois	Pawnee
Anadarko	Iowa	Peoria
Apache	Kaskaskia	Piankashaw
Apalachicola	Kansa	Ponca
Arapaho	Kichai	Potawatomi
Caddo	Kickapoo	Quapaw
Cahokia	Kiowa	Sauk and Fox
Catawba	Kiowa-Apache	Seminole
Cayuga	Koasati	Seneca
Cherokee	Lipan	Shawnee
Cheyenne	Miami	Skidi
Chickasaw	Michigamea	Stockbridge
Chippewa	Modoc	Tamaroa
Choctaw	Mohawk	Tawakoni
Comanche	Moingwena	Tonkawa
Conestoga	Munsee	Tuscarora
Creek	Natchez	Tuskegee
Delaware	Nez Percé	Waco
Eel River	Osage	Wea
Erie	Oto and Missouri	Wichita
Hainai	Ottawa	Wyandot
Hitchiti		Yuchi

Table 2. Population Summary
American Indians, All Races, Oklahoma and United States
1970

	Oklahoma Indian	Oklahoma All Races	U.S. Indian	U.S. All Races
Total population	96,803	2,559,175	763,594	203,210,150
Percent urban	49.2	68.0	44.6	73.5
Percent rural	50.8	32.0	55.4	26.5
Median age (Years)	23.2	29.0	20.4	28.1
Family size	4.12	3.36	4.70	3.57

Source: *American Indians*: 1970 Census of Population, Bureau of the Census PC (2)–1F.

Table 3.   Categories of Indian Descent in Oklahoma, 1970

Category	Estimated Number
Sociocultural Indians	100,000
Legal Indians	220,000
Individuals of Indian descent	600,000

Table 4. Reported Indian Population in Oklahoma, 1900-70

Year	Number	Change
1900	64,445	
1910	74,825	+10,380
1920	56,337	−17,488
1930	92,725	+35,388
1940	63,125	−29,600
1950	55,769	− 7,356
1960	64,689	+ 8,920
1970	96,731	+33,042

Table 5.   Indian Population by County, April 1970

County	Population, All Races	Population, Indian	Indian Percentage of Total
Adair	15,141	4,150	27.4
Alfalfa	7,224	33	0.5
Atoka	10,972	582	5.3
Beaver	6,282	7	0.1
Beckham	15,754	137	0.9
Blaine	11,794	801	6.8
Bryan	25,552	1,030	4.0
Caddo	28,931	4,080	14.1
Canadian	32,245	1,168	3.6
Carter	37,349	1,070	2.9
Cherokee	23,174	4,418	19.1
Choctaw	15,141	908	6.0
Cimarron	4,145	12	0.3
Cleveland	81,839	1,524	1.9
Coal	5,525	437	7.9
Comanche	108,144	3,343	3.1
Cotton	6,832	337	4.9
Craig	14,722	891	6.1
Creek	45,532	1,913	4.2
Custer	22,665	800	3.5
Delaware	17,767	3,511	19.2
Dewey	5,656	253	4.5
Ellis	5,129	18	0.4
Garfield	56,343	436	0.8
Garvin	24,874	492	2.0
Grady	29,354	355	1.2
Grant	7,114	35	0.5
Greer	7,979	77	1.0
Harmon	5,136	22	0.4
Harper	5,151	27	0.5
Haskell	9,578	428	4.5
Hughes	13,228	1,520	11.5
Jackson	30,902	226	0.7
Jefferson	7,125	52	0.7

County	Population, All Races	Population, Indian	Indian Percentage of Total
Johnston	7,870	615	7.8
Kay	48,791	1,865	3.8
Kingfisher	12,857	257	2.0
Kiowa	12,532	490	3.9
Latimer	8,601	714	8.3
Le Flore	32,137	1,406	4.4
Lincoln	19,482	292	1.5
Logan	19,645	116	0.6
Love	5,637	107	1.9
McClain	14,157	226	1.6
McCurtain	28,642	2,493	8.7
McIntosh	12,472	1,550	12.4
Major	7,529	27	0.4
Marshall	7,682	330	4.3
Mayes	23,302	2,496	10.7
Murray	10,669	470	4.4
Muskogee	59,542	3,022	5.1
Noble	10,043	474	4.7
Nowata	9,773	423	4.3
Okfuskee	10,683	1,278	12.0
Oklahoma	527,717	10,341	2.0
Okmulgee	35,358	2,147	6.1
Osage	29,750	2,565	8.6
Ottawa	29,800	2,055	6.9
Pawnee	11,338	783	6.9
Payne	50,654	626	1.2
Pittsburg	37,521	1,541	4.1
Pontotoc	27,867	1,313	4.7
Pottawatomie	43,134	2,017	4.7
Pushmataha	9,385	654	7.0
Roger Mills	4,452	294	6.6
Rogers	28,425	1,672	5.9
Seminole	25,144	2,643	10.5
Sequoyah	23,370	2,037	8.7

County	Population, All Races	Population, Indian	Indian Percentage of Total
Stephens	35,902	476	1.3
Texas	16,352	50	0.3
Tillman	12,901	233	1.8
Tulsa	399,982	11,041	2.8
Wagoner	22,163	799	3.6
Washington	42,302	1,241	2.9
Washita	12,141	103	0.8
Woods	11,920	31	0.3
Woodward	15,537	61	0.4
Totals	2,559,460	98,468	

Source: *Indians in Oklahoma:* June, 1975, Research and Planning Division, Oklahoma Employment Security Commission, Oklahoma City.

MAPS

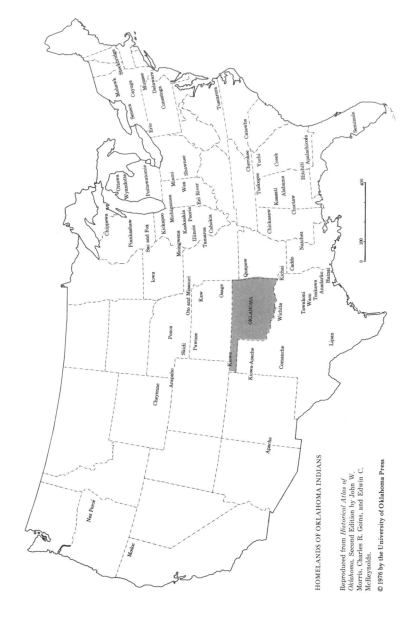

HOMELANDS OF OKLAHOMA INDIANS

Reproduced from *Historical Atlas of Oklahoma*, Second Edition by John W. Morris, Charles R. Goins, and Edwin C. McReynolds.

© 1976 by the University of Oklahoma Press

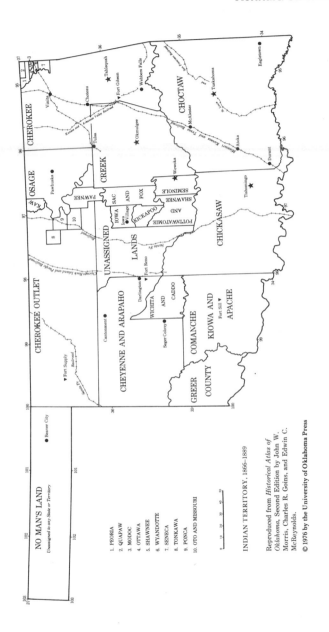

INDIAN TERRITORY, 1866–1889

Reproduced from *Historical Atlas of Oklahoma*, Second Edition by John W. Morris, Charles R. Goins, and Edwin C. McReynolds.

© 1976 by the University of Oklahoma Press

169

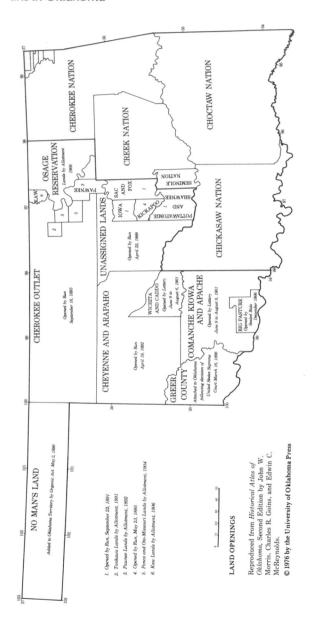

NO MAN'S LAND

Added to Oklahoma Territory by Organic Act May 2, 1890

CHEROKEE OUTLET

*Opened by Run
September 16, 1893*

CHEROKEE NATION

OSAGE RESERVATION

*Lands by Allotment
1906*

KAW 6

PAWNEE 3

5

5

2

CREEK NATION

CHOCTAW NATION

UNASSIGNED LANDS

*Opened by Run
April 22, 1889*

IOWA 1

SAC AND FOX 2

SHAWNEE

POTTAWATOMIE AND

KICKAPOO 4

SEMINOLE NATION

CHEYENNE AND ARAPAHO

*Opened by Run
April 19, 1892*

WICHITA AND CADDO

*Opened by Lottery
June 9 to
August 6, 1901*

COMANCHE KIOWA AND APACHE

*Opened by Lottery
June 9 to August 6, 1901*

CHICKASAW NATION

GREER COUNTY

*Attached to Oklahoma
following decision of
United States Supreme
Court March 16, 1896*

BIG PASTURE

*Opened by
Sealed Bids
December 1906*

LAND OPENINGS

1. *Opened by Run, September 22, 1891*
2. *Tonkawa Lands by Allotment, 1891*
3. *Pawnee Lands by Allotment, 1892*
4. *Opened by Run, May 23, 1895*
5. *Ponca and Oto-Missouri Lands by Allotment, 1904*
6. *Kaw Lands by Allotment, 1906*

0 10 20 30 40 50

Reproduced from *Historical Atlas of
Oklahoma*, Second Edition by John W.
Morris, Charles R. Goins, and Edwin C.
McReynolds.
© 1976 by the University of Oklahoma Press

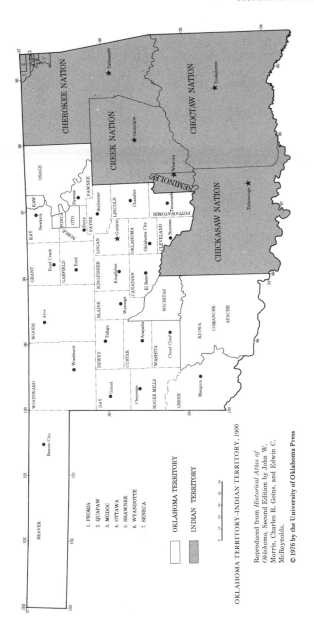

OKLAHOMA TERRITORY-INDIAN TERRITORY, 1900

1. PEORIA
2. QUAPAW
3. MODOC
4. OTTAWA
5. SHAWNEE
6. WYANDOTTE
7. SENECA

☐ OKLAHOMA TERRITORY

▨ INDIAN TERRITORY

Reproduced from *Historical Atlas of Oklahoma*, Second Edition by John W. Morris, Charles R. Goins, and Edwin C. McReynolds.

© 1976 by the University of Oklahoma Press